Diseases and Disorders

Down Syndrome

Titles in the Diseases and Disorder series include:

Diseases and Disorders

Down Syndrome

by Christina M. Girod

Library of Congress Cataloging-in-Publication Data

Girod, Christina M.
    Down syndrome / by Christina M. Girod.
      p. cm. — (Diseases and disorders series)
    Includes bibliographical references and index.
      ISBN 1-56006-824-8 (hardcover : alk. paper)
    1. Down syndrome—Juvenile literature. [1. Down syndrome. 2. Mentally handicapped.] I. Title. II. Series.
RJ506.D68 G58   2001
616.85'8842—dc21   00-009933

Table of Contents

"The Most Difficult Puzzles Ever Devised"

Charles Best, one of the pioneers in the search for a cure for diabetes, once explained what it is about medical research that intrigued him so. "It's not just the gratification of knowing one is helping people," he confided, "although that probably is a more heroic and selfless motivation. Those feelings may enter in, but truly, what I find best is the feeling of going toe to toe with nature, of trying to solve the most difficult puzzles ever devised. The answers are there somewhere, those keys that will solve the puzzle and make the patient well. But how will those keys be found?"

Since the dawn of civilization, nothing has so puzzled people—and often frightened them, as well—as the onset of illness in a body or mind that had seemed healthy before. A seizure, the inability of a heart to pump, the sudden deterioration of muscle tone in a small child—being unable to reverse such conditions or even to understand why they occur was unspeakably frustrating to healers. Even before there were names for such conditions, even before they were understood at all, each was a reminder of how complex the human body was, and how vulnerable.

While our grappling with understanding diseases has been frustrating at times, it has also provided some of humankind's most heroic accomplishments. Alexander Fleming's accidental discovery in 1928 of a mold that could be turned into penicillin has resulted in the saving of untold millions of lives. The isolation of the enzyme insulin has reversed what was once a death sentence for anyone with diabetes. There have been great strides in combating conditions for which there is not yet a cure, too. Medicines can help AIDS patients live longer, diagnostic tools such as mammography and ultrasounds can help doctors find tumors while they are treatable, and laser surgery techniques have made the most intricate, minute operations routine.

This "toe-to-toe" competition with diseases and disorders is even more remarkable when seen in a historical continuum. An astonishing amount of progress has been made in a very short time. Just two hundred years ago, the existence of germs as a cause of some diseases was unknown. In fact, it was less than 150 years ago that a British surgeon named Joseph Lister had difficulty persuading his fellow doctors that washing their hands before delivering a baby might increase the chances of a healthy delivery (especially if they had just attended to a diseased patient)!

Each book in Lucent's *Diseases and Disorders* series explores a disease or disorder and the knowledge that has been accumulated (or discarded) by doctors through the years. Each book also examines the tools used for pinpointing a diagnosis, as well as the various means that are used to treat or cure a disease. Finally, new ideas are presented—techniques or medicines that may be on the horizon.

Frustration and disappointment are still part of medicine, for not every disease or condition can be cured or prevented. But the limitations of knowledge are being pushed outward constantly; the "most difficult puzzles ever devised" are finding challengers every day.

The Road to Acceptance

WHEN JASON KINGSLEY was born with Down syndrome in 1974, the doctor told his parents, "He'll never sit or stand, walk or talk. He'll never be able to distinguish you from any other adults. He'll never read or write or have a single meaningful thought or idea."[1] He told them to place Jason in an institution and then go home and tell their family he had died at birth. Jason's story is not uncommon, for up until the 1970s it was common practice to put a baby with Down syndrome in an institution immediately, with the family guarding their carefully kept secret.

Fortunately for Jason, his family ignored this doctor's advice. Instead, they took Jason home and worked hard to make sure he got a good education. He became an advocate for people with Down syndrome while still a child: He was one of the first disabled children to appear on nationwide television, with a part on *Sesame Street* and later roles in several other television shows. When Jason graduated from high school in New York state in 1994, he took and passed the state competency tests required for all "normal" students to graduate. Jason graduated with a regular high school diploma. Today he works on behalf of disabled people all over the United States and is striving to live completely on his own.

What is Down Syndrome?

Down syndrome is a genetic disorder. That means that it is caused by abnormalities in a person's genes. However, Down syndrome is not inherited, meaning that parents do not pass the condition to their children. No one really knows what causes Down syndrome, but scientists are working diligently to answer this question. They are also studying how this disorder affects the genes. They are using the information they discover to develop a treatment for Down syndrome, which they hope will be available in the near future.

People with Down syndrome are easily identified by their facial features.

Most people today recognize a person who has Down syndrome by the characteristic facial features. These features include slightly slanted eyes with small skin folds at the inner corner of the eyes, a flattened nasal bridge, a short neck, and a tongue that tends to protrude. In addition, people who have Down syndrome are often born with health problems: Heart defects affect 40 percent of those with the disorder, and most have poor muscle tone. They are also prone to get certain diseases or conditions, such as respiratory infections or leukemia. The most significant symptom of Down syndrome, however, is mental retardation. Most children with Down syndrome have mild or moderate mental retardation, which affects their cognitive (thinking), social, language, and motor development.

When people with Down syndrome become adults they have many options available to meet their individual needs. They may live alone, with roommates, with family members, or with a spouse. More often than not they have jobs and enjoy the same parks, museums, theaters, and other recreational activities that everyone else does. Some adults with Down syndrome need help with caring for their personal, legal, financial, or health needs, while others are able to take responsibility for some of their own affairs.

Becoming a Part of Society

Since the 1970s, a growing number of children, like Jason, are living at home instead of in institutions and are receiving appropriate education. As a result, the 1990s saw the greatest number of independent and semi-independent, educated, working adults with Down syndrome to date. Today they are more accepted by society and are more likely to be viewed as contributing citizens of their communities.

Acceptance did not come overnight, however. Parents had to fight so their children with Down syndrome could go to school like other children. In the 1970s laws were passed that protected the right of children with Down syndrome, as well as those with other disabilities, to attend public school. Parents also had to fight to have their children with Down syndrome allowed to participate in their communities—it was not uncommon in those days for restaurant and store managers to ask families to leave "because the other customers might be bothered" by the presence of a child with Down syndrome. Today children and adults with Down syndrome enjoy themselves at theaters, eat at restaurants, and shop in stores, right alongside nondisabled persons.

Adults with Down syndrome are increasingly working in regular jobs in the community, rather than being segregated from the public eye in supervised workshops where only other disabled persons work. Treatment research, educating the public about Down syndrome, and, most importantly, helping people with Down syndrome become as independent and self-sufficient as possible will go a long way toward the goal of wholly integrating them into society.

Chapter 1

The History of Down Syndrome

B EN IS A young man in his mid-twenties who lives with several "buddies" in a small house in Maryland. He works at the local grocery store and spends much of his free time going to movies, hanging out at the pizza place, and just chatting with friends. He loves to watch *Looney Tunes* on television and play old Beatles hits when he needs his spirits lifted. In many ways Ben is like other young, single adults just starting out in life. But Ben is different: He has Down syndrome. Not so long ago, Ben's independent lifestyle would have been impossible. Up until about 1970, people like Ben had few choices and fewer opportunities to grow up at home surrounded by mom, dad, brothers, and sisters, to go to school, to get a job, and to live on their own.

Nearly everyone encounters people like Ben somewhere at sometime. Ben's mother, Marilyn, is grateful for the more "enlightened" society that has allowed him to develop into the independent person he is, but she notes that it has taken many uphill battles to get there. Even now, she finds that Ben must prove that he is worthy to be a part of society, as Marilyn describes in an essay:

> Most people we chance to meet know little or nothing about Down syndrome. . . . We can't be sure what goes on in the heads of those who encounter our kids. Strangers anywhere and everywhere: the shopping center, Joe's Pizza Parlor, the Ice Capades, the next block. Whether our child with Down syndrome is yet a cute little four-year-old or a young adult, he or she is still going to be looked at, inspected . . . by strangers. . . . I'm convinced, this

"inspection" will be from a prejudged, prejudiced, biased—call it
what you will—point of view.[2]

Much of this prejudice Marilyn speaks of is caused by fear. People have always feared the different, that which they are unfamiliar with and possibly do not understand. And avoiding or shunning that which is different is a way some people protect themselves from the unknown. Persons who have Down syndrome do not always speak appropriately to strangers, and sometimes act inappropriately in public. This is because persons with Down syndrome also have mental retardation, which means that their intellectual ability is below the average of most other people of the same age. Down syndrome affects a person in many ways, but the most significant effect it causes is mental retardation. Mental retardation affects the way a person learns, makes friends, and the kind of work he or she is able to do, but it does not affect a person's ability to love or to be happy.

Because mental retardation affects people with Down syndrome so profoundly, throughout history these men, women, and children have been misunderstood, mistreated, and isolated. Not until about one hundred and fifty years ago did anyone begin to notice that Down syndrome existed, and then to study it.

Invisible Population

Early doctors and scientists did not understand that many different disorders can cause mental retardation; Down syndrome is just one. Fragile X syndrome (also a genetic condition), and fetal alcohol syndrome (caused by excessive drinking during pregnancy), cause mental retardation as well. However, all these syndromes were lumped into one big group. Doctors and scientists had little interest in mental retardation or its causes until approximately the mid-1800s because other problems that affected greater numbers of people, like malnutrition and infections, demanded their attention.

People with Down syndrome were treated much the same way that others with mental retardation were treated. Feared and misunderstood, they were shunned by society and treated as if they were less than human. They were also less visible to the general public than they are today, for babies born with Down syndrome often died as infants, and those who survived were usually hidden by their families or sent away to institutions. However, as people came to value life more, a few observant scientists and doctors began to notice common physical characteristics some people with mental retardation shared. This knowledge prompted other scientists to study the disorder that eventually came to be known as Down syndrome.

A Distinct and Separate Entity

In 1866, Édouard Séguin, a French physician and one of the first educators to open a school for the mentally retarded, recorded a description of a patient whose physical features were suggestive of Down syndrome. These features were described as "milk-white, rosy, and peeling skin . . . with its cracked lips and tongue; [and] the . . . skin at the margin of the lids [eyes]."[3] Séguin noticed that several students in his school had a similar appearance and called the condition "furfuraceous [scaly] idiocy," in reference to the dry skin that many of them had.

Another medical researcher described in 1866 a girl "with a small round head, Chinese looking eyes, projecting a large tongue

Children with Down syndrome are no longer isolated from society. Many, like these preschoolers, enjoy activities with other children.

who only knew a few words."[4] Gradually more and more trained observers were beginning to discuss the common characteristics that some people with mental retardation shared. That same year, John Langdon Down, a medical practitioner in England, noticed the common physical features of several mentally retarded persons involved in his study. He published a paper that for the first time described in detail the physical characteristics of the condition that would later bear his name.

Down's paper was the first to distinguish Down syndrome children from others who exhibited mental retardation. Down reported, "the hair is . . . straight and scanty. The face is flat and broad. The eyes are obliquely placed [slanted]. The nose is small. These children have considerable power of imitation [great ability to copy what others do]."[5] Because of the almond -shaped appearance of the eyes in such children, he called the condition "mongolian idiocy." At this time the word *Mongolian* was used to refer to persons of Asian descent, who also have almond-shaped eyes. Although he inaccurately compared the features of Down syndrome to Asian features, his descriptions were significant in that they described a whole group rather than just one individual.

All in a Name

Eventually the condition became known as "mongolism," and those who had it were called "mongoloids" or "mongolian idiots." For decades the words *idiocy* and *idiot* were commonly used by the scientific and medical community to describe Down syndrome and the people who had it, as well as other mentally retarded persons. Although the terms were not intended to be degrading they were used by others to mock those who had Down syndrome, sparking objections from many family members. Despite the fact that these terms were insensitive, they were used for more than a century, as Marilyn Trainer attests to in this recounting of a doctor's visit in the late 1960s when Ben was two months old:

> The physician carefully positioned his hand under Ben's small belly and lifted him from the examining table. Ben's arms and legs dangled down and I heard the words, "Here you see the typical Mongol with the problem of hypotonia [poor muscle tone]. Notice

the lack of firm muscle tone in the arms, legs, and neck, and notice the tonguing. Most Mongoloids exhibit these characteristics, which are often the first clues in the diagnosis of Mongolism."[6]

It was not until the 1960s when both Asian people as well as parents of children with Down syndrome protested the use of these terms that a new name was sought. In response the medical community chose to name the condition "Down's Syndrome" in honor of John Langdon Down. Later the final "s" was dropped to become the term "Down syndrome" used today.

Once Down syndrome was identified as a separate and distinct disorder, scientists wanted to find out what caused it. All manner of reasons were cited as the cause, from poor nutrition to maternal alcoholism. Researcher G. E. Shuttleworth's explanation of the cause of Down syndrome in 1886 illustrated a popular, although incorrect, theory of the time—that Down syndrome occurred when a child did not completely develop. Shuttleworth wrote that "their peculiar appearance [was] really that of a phase of fetal life."[7]

Natural Selection and the Rise of Institutions

Near the end of the nineteenth century, Charles Darwin's theories of evolution became the basis for a seriously flawed approach to Down syndrome. One of Darwin's ideas was that of natural selection,

which means that members of a group with traits that allow them to adapt better to their environment reproduce in greater numbers than those who have less favorable traits. When some people attempted to fit Down syndrome into the natural selection framework, they concluded that the syndrome's less favorable

Charles Darwin's ideas influenced the belief that children with Down syndrome were not fit to be a part of society.

traits, such as lower intellectual abilities, meant that people with Down syndrome were less capable than others of adapting to their environment (school, family life, or work) and thus were not well equipped to survive and reproduce. This line of reasoning was used to justify treating persons with Down syndrome like primitive throwbacks who had failed to evolve as highly as the rest of humankind. In a misguided effort to preserve the process of natural selection, children with Down syndrome were regularly sent away to institutions for the mentally retarded and segregated from the rest of society.

Up until the 1980s some of these institutions continued to exist, underfunded and understaffed. In fact, some were so deplorable that they were considered scandals. One such institution was profiled in a 1970s news story: "[they showed] 'residents' sitting on the floor doing nothing, up against a wall banging their heads, curled motionless on a bed, wandering down corridors screeching, or standing quietly waiting for someone—anyone— who never comes. . . . [There are] stark 'recreation areas.'"[8]

The Ability to Learn

Although such inhuman, warehouse-type institutions existed solely to keep Down syndrome persons separate from the public, some health care professionals attempted to educate or train the residents. An early-nineteenth-century French physician, Jean-Marc-Gaspard Itard, was the first person who promoted the idea that mentally retarded persons, including those with Down syndrome, could be educated. He believed that a person's development was wholly dependent on the environment in which he lived. This meant that a child who grows up without books, toys, people to talk with, pictures on the wall, and crayons, paints, clay, and other creative materials would not learn as much or as easily as a child who enjoyed such an enriched environment. One parent remembers how such a sterile life affected a neighborhood girl who had Down syndrome:

> Growing up . . . I used to walk home past this one girl who was not in school. Every day when I walked by, she used to say, "You have long hair." I remember feeling very uncomfortable. I was a little afraid of her. Now, when I think back, I know that

she obviously had a lot of potential—she could relate to others and all—but she just had nothing to do all day long.[9]

Itard believed that if he changed the environment—the home or the school—to make it interesting and full of challenging activities, children with Down syndrome would prove to be capable of learning. Itard's ideas were supported by scientific studies during the 1930s and 1940s that concluded stimulating environments were more conducive to learning. Even so, up until the 1960s most Down syndrome children were placed in institutions at birth upon the advice of a doctor. Although some children received training at such institutions, many suffered from the lack of love, attention, and security provided by home and family. Eventually concerned parents and educators, alarmed by the inadequacies of custodial facilities, began to resist institutionalization of Down syndrome children. Rather, they insisted that the home was the best place for them to grow up, surrounded by loved ones, involved in the community, and attending school.

Mara, a young woman with Down syndrome, attended a regular school and grew up with her family in her own home, surrounded by people who cared about her. Mara can read and write, and she

A girl with Down syndrome plays Monopoly with her brother. Studies show that such interaction helps Down syndrome children lead more independent lives.

enjoys spending time with friends. She lives in a group home with three others who also have Down syndrome, and works as a clerk at a nearby video rental store. Obviously, the simple investment of time and attention benefited Mara's development.

Fortunately Itard's ideas have resulted in brighter futures for thousands of Down syndrome children like Mara. But for many doctors, enhancing the lives of those with this disorder was not enough. A handful of dedicated physicians wanted to find out what caused Down syndrome and why. Was it a genetic disorder? Could it be prevented?

An Extra Chromosome

In the 1930s, based on the nineteenth-century genetics research by Gregor Mendel, scientists first speculated that Down syndrome might be the result of a defect in the genes. However, technology was too limited at the time to allow the study of genetics, so Mendel's ideas could not be tested.

Finally in 1956 a powerful microscope that enabled researchers to view genetic material became available, and some of the mystery surrounding the cause of Down syndrome began to be solved. A French physician, Jerome Lejeune, used this powerful microscope to look at human chromosomes, the long strands of DNA that hold a person's

Theories that Down syndrome is caused by defective genes are based on the research of Gregor Mendel.

genes. In every cell he was able to see individual chromosomes, and he noticed that there was always the same number of chromosomes in each cell. Lejeune counted twenty-three pairs, for a total of forty-six chromosomes in normal human cells. Then in 1959 he decided to look at the cells of Down syndrome patients.

He found that persons with Down syndrome had an extra chromosome, for a total of forty-seven in each cell. Moreover, he discovered that the extra strand was chromosome number 21, meaning that instead of the normal pair, there were three copies of chromosome 21 in each cell. This led him to call the condition trisomy 21 (*tri-* meaning three, and *-somy* for chromosome).

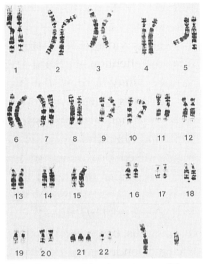

An extra strand in chromosome 21 causes Down syndrome.

Although Lejeune had completed one part of the puzzle, there were still several questions that lingered. What caused the extra chromosome? How did the presence of the extra chromosome affect a person's body at the cellular level? These are questions that scientists are still struggling to answer today. In the meantime others in the medical community have devoted themselves to finding a way to prevent or reverse the effects of Down syndrome.

Metabolic Miracle?

In the 1950s a physician in Michigan, Henry Turkel, developed an approach for treating Down syndrome children. His idea was to use drugs and nutrition to compensate for problems of metabolism, that is, disorders in the body's chemical processing of substances. Turkel believed that mental retardation was not present at birth but developed over time as a result of brain damage due to a lack of oxygen in the body's cells. The lack of oxygen, in turn, was attributed to the metabolic problems often present in Down syndrome patients. The combination of nutrients and drugs Turkel used was called the U-series, and it included vitamins, minerals, fatty acids, digestive enzymes, amino acids, thyroid hormone, antihistamines, and nasal decongestants. Turkel believed these nutrients and drugs would help increase the oxygen in Down syndrome children's cells, preventing mental retardation and improving unfavorable medical conditions.

Scores of parents claimed that the U-series improved their children's language skills, expanded their creativity, and enhanced their reading abilities. Moreover, many said their children's physical condition also improved, including muscle tone, skin condition, and eyesight problems. Studies were later conducted where one group of Down syndrome patients received the U-series and another group was given a placebo (an inactive substance, which patients—or in this case, parents—believe to be the treatment being tested). Despite parents' claims of success, these studies showed no significant improvement in the physical or mental condition of those in the group that received the actual U-series. As a result, Turkel's treatments were not well accepted by either the scientific and medical community or the federal government.

Although Turkel's U-series has not been used since the 1980s, his work drew attention to the mental and physical condition of children with Down syndrome. Since Turkel first developed his nutritional treatment, much more has been learned about how this disorder affects the development of these children and what can be done to help them master developmental challenges from walking and talking to making friends and keeping themselves healthy.

Chapter 2

Development with Down Syndrome

One morning when Ben was barely past two, he toddled into the kitchen and found me sweeping the floor. He observed me for a moment and I saw him glance around the room. Then he toddled over to the kitchen closet, opened the door, reached in to pull out the dust pan, and brought it to me. Next he bent down and held it near the broom. I was dumbfounded, and then oh, how I wanted to pick him up . . . and go dancing around the kitchen! . . . What Ben had done was not just something "cute" in passing. What Ben had done was to *observe*—to *remember*—to *anticipate*— to *put it all together*—and then act upon it. This was *thinking*. . . . Beyond any doubt my little boy could *think!* [10]

CHILDREN THINK AND act in all sorts of ways every day. But when a child with Down syndrome, like Ben, "puts it all together," families celebrate a major milestone. Children with Down syndrome have to work much harder than their nondisabled peers to learn to walk, talk, ride a bike, read, and even to know that when mom sweeps up a pile of dust, a dustpan is needed to collect it. Down syndrome also affects the rate at which children develop, which is usually slower than average. However, rates of development vary a great deal even among children with Down syndrome.

Growth

Three-year-old Josh weighs just twenty-three pounds and stands barely tall enough to meet the shoulders of his thirty-five-pound

Children with Down syndrome develop physically at a much slower rate than other children in part due to problems associated with swallowing, hormone deficiencies and heart conditions.

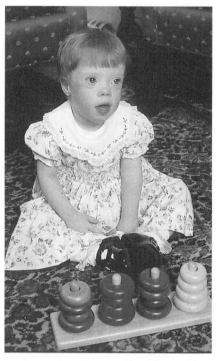

classmates in preschool. As he grows up, he will probably not get taller than a little over five feet and will be shorter than most of his classmates through high school. Josh, who has Down syndrome, suffered from undernourishment as a baby and has an underactive thyroid gland, which causes him to grow more slowly than his peers. Josh had feeding problems early in life that contributed to the lack of nourishment; during his first year he had difficulty swallowing and was not able to consume everything his mother fed him. Later, when he began to eat solid foods, he still could not swallow very well, and he continued to gain weight and grow very slowly.

Like Josh, many children with Down syndrome fall behind their peers in height and fail to gain weight as young children. Often this is due to malnourishment, caused by such conditions as Josh's swallowing problems. Hormone deficiencies and heart conditions are also common birth defects in children with Down syndrome.

Ironically, many of these children are overweight by the time they are teenagers. This is frequently caused by poor eating habits, such as overindulgence in high-calorie, high-fat foods, combined with a slow metabolism. Marilyn Trainer believes children with Down syndrome, like her son Ben, may use food to keep some control over choices in their lives, as she explains:

Like most good Americans, Ben is enamored of french fries, hamburgers, ice cream, and soft drinks. Every chance he gets, Ben partakes of foods he knows we discourage him from eating. When given the opportunity, he eats these foods even if he's not hungry. . . . Unless he is self-motivated to control his own food habits, he is going to indulge himself. Allen and I can attempt to reason with him until we turn blue in the face.[11]

Some parents even allow overindulgence in food as a way of "making up" for any unhappiness associated with not being able to achieve at the same rate other children do. The practice is ill-advised, however, because it aggravates a condition that affects a large proportion of children with Down syndrome: poor muscle tone.

Motor Development and Self-Help Skills

Many babies with Down syndrome are born with poor muscle tone, causing the weak muscles Marilyn Trainer noted when Ben was an infant. This shortcoming makes it difficult for babies with Down syndrome to use their arms and legs the way other babies do when learning to grasp objects, and later to crawl and walk. All-important milestones in motor development include the use of arms, hands, legs, and other parts of the body to do certain things, from picking up a Cheerio with the thumb and finger to riding a bike or tying shoelaces.

Often the physical or medical problems some children are born with delay motor development. As with growth rates, malnourishment and heart defects can hinder the development of motor skills. One parent describes the frustration of her child's attempts to achieve skills using a ball: "His hand-eye and motor coordination aren't that hot. He's done a lot better in the past year or so, but for the longest time he had problems catching a ball, kicking the ball properly. If he was playing baseball or something, he had a hard time hitting the ball. He gets frustrated a lot."[12]

Motor skills are necessary for learning self-help skills, which enable a person to do personal care activities such as feeding, dressing, bathing, and using the toilet unassisted. Self-feeding might not seem a daunting task, but children must pick up a spoon, scoop the food onto the spoon, bring it to their mouth

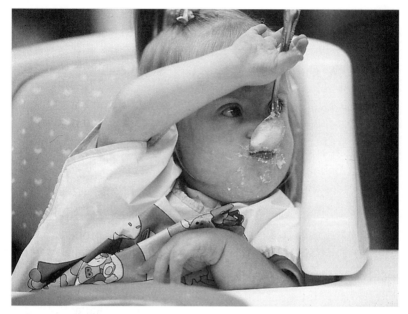

Many Down syndrome children receive help with motor-skill development, a necessary step in building coordination.

without spilling, and finally place the spoon in their open mouth. Think of how challenging these steps are for a normal two-year-old, and then how doubly difficult it would be for a child with Down syndrome. Today many children with Down syndrome begin receiving help in motor development at an early age. Special exercises and activities may help improve muscle tone and coordination. Furthermore, in achieving motor skills, children make a mental plan of action. For example, an infant who wants to reach a toy a couple of feet away will make a subconscious plan to get the toy. This could involve rolling over, a motor skill developed at about five months of age. This skill requires the infant to think subconsciously how to move the body to achieve this result. Mental planning requires cognitive, or thinking, skills.

Cognitive Development

Cognitive development includes problem solving, critical thinking, abstract thinking, and memory. Children with Down syndrome may have stronger skills in some cognitive areas than in others. Ricky's experiences with different ways of studying arithmetic are typical.

On some days Ricky learns very easily and is turned on by what he is learning. Yet other days he seems uninterested. Ricky learned to use a calculator without difficulty, and he learned to add much faster when the numbers were prices on a menu than he did when presented with a photocopied sheet full of addition problems. As one of his parents explains: "Motivation and attention are everything in his education, and he doesn't care about learning abstract numbers that do not relate to things in his life. But he does care about learning to read a fast food menu and to add the prices on it."[13]

Many children with Down syndrome have problems with memory, but, like Ricky, they are better able to remember what they have learned when it has meaning to them. Moreover, memory is affected by the ability to pay attention to what one is learning. For example, Ricky was interested in the calculator and so was able to focus enough attention on it to learn to use it quickly. However, he was not interested in the page full of addition problems and probably did not pay much attention to the instructions. Thus, he found it difficult to learn and remember the skill of adding in the traditional way.

Many children with Down syndrome also have difficulty in problem solving. Jill, who has Down syndrome, wants to play with a doll that is sitting on a high shelf. She tries reaching for the doll but is not tall enough. Rather than finding another way to get

Difficulty with memory and problem solving pose special challenges for children with Down syndrome.

the doll, Jill just keeps on trying to reach it and grows more and more frustrated. Her friend Bobby tries to reach the doll too, but cannot. However, Bobby, who does not have Down syndrome, is able to think of a different way to solve the problem. He brings a stool over, stands on it, and gets the doll for Jill.

Similarly, many children with Down syndrome lack foresight about the consequences of their actions. As with problem solving, they may not see more than one possible outcome or option. Marilyn Trainer illustrates this in a story about Ben:

Several hours later [Ben and Paul, a friend] were back grumbling with indignation about something and commiserating with each other.

"What's wrong?" I asked. "Didn't you like the movie?"

"It was great!"

"Then what's wrong? Did you have trouble buying your tickets?"

"No, Laura [another friend] bought our tickets."

"Do you mean she paid for them or did you give her money to buy them?"

"She bought them with her own money. . . . BUT SHE WOULDN'T SHARE THE POPCORN!"

"Who bought the popcorn?"

"Laura bought the popcorn . . . but she wouldn't share it!"

. . . The only thing [they] could think about was that Laura had refused to share the popcorn. The fact that she had paid for their tickets didn't phase them; in fact, it didn't register with them at all. . . .

"Hey you guys," I asked, "didn't you have your wallets with you and didn't you have money in those wallets?"

"Yes," they answered. . . .

"Well, you both had money, so why didn't you go to the refreshment stand *and buy your own popcorn?*"

Surely there was no more illumination . . . than in the light bulbs which simultaneously went on above their heads. They looked at me in astonishment and admiration.

"What a great idea!" Ben said.

"Next time we'll do that!" Paul said.[14]

Another common problem in cognitive development for children with Down syndrome is the ability to generalize—to apply what they have learned in one situation to another situation. One parent explains:

Sometimes Ricky will not be able to do something—read or write a word, add some numbers, or type something on the computer—that I have seen him do several times before. . . . Maybe Ricky gets derailed by slightly different situations or contexts in which questions are asked. Maybe sometimes how he is asked trips him up.[15]

Cognitive development affects a child's ability to learn how to behave appropriately in social situations as well. The ability to generalize, solve problems, and foresee consequences plays a major role in social development.

Social Development

Children with Down syndrome may experience difficulties in social situations. Younger children tend to play more alongside other children rather than with them. Moreover, children with Down syndrome often look to their peers for guidance in play situations. Laurie is a six-year-old with Down syndrome whose parents often bring her to a neighbor's house on weekends so that she has the opportunity to play with other children. Usually Laurie heads straight for the playhouse, and although the other children try to include her, she can often be seen "cooking" alone in the kitchen while her playmates discuss a trip to the park. There is very little interaction between Laurie and the other children unless they ask her to join them and actually guide her actions (such as pushing the stroller).

Young children with Down syndrome also prefer routines and like to repeat the same type of play over and over again. This is illustrated by one parent's story:

[W]hen our son was real small, he would take his little cars and line them up in a row. If you walked by and made one of those cars move a fraction of an inch, he went crazy. He wanted that line right there, in perfect order. Also, he would never build with building blocks; he lined them up. Even when the psychologist would try to get him to build stacks, he'd just line them up like a train, no building. . . . Everything had to be a certain way, and if you deviated from that, he couldn't handle it. He did not like change at all.[16]

Children with Down syndrome need a great deal of guidance and support in learning good manners, sharing, approaching other children, maintaining play, and being responsible for their own behavior and belongings. Giving them opportunities to practice these skills in school, restaurants, stores, and other public places can enhance their social development and improve self-confidence. Confidence is an important consideration because some children with Down syndrome are aware of the differences between themselves and their peers. They may even realize when others are making fun of them or avoiding them, although they may not fully understand why. Such experiences may lead to a negative self-image and low confidence in social situations.

Plenty of practice in social situations early in life is especially important for the teen years, when peer groups are so crucial to identity. Teens with Down syndrome often find themselves avoided by classmates because they do not seem to know how to behave like everyone else. In conversation, they may get too close to someone's face, or repeat the same joke or complaint over and over within a short period of time. They may approach total strangers with a hug or other inappropriate display of affection. "We can go to a grocery store and he'll go up and start talking to someone," explains one parent. "We get various reactions. We've had some really good reactions and we've had some really horrendous reactions. He doesn't seem to pick up on the negative in the bad reactions, though."[17] Timing is another problem, as when a teen with Down syndrome approaches a coworker and strikes up a conversation about his favorite music group while customers are waiting to be helped.

In addition, difficulties in critical thinking may make teens with Down syndrome gullible. "She is very outgoing and friendly," said one parent, "but people could take advantage of her too. She is not very discerning. She needs support . . . she would pay $10,000 for something that costs $10."[18]

Social development of children with Down syndrome is also affected by how well a child communicates with others because language is the basis of social interaction.

Being able to play and interact with other children is crucial in a Down syndrome child's social development.

Language Development

Children with Down syndrome are doubly challenged when it comes to language development. Not only is their speech affected by a variety of physical problems, but language may be delayed due to cognitive challenges as well.

Physical problems such as poor muscle tone in the face or mouth or a frequently protruding tongue can hinder a child's ability to form intelligible speech sounds. Moreover, hearing impairments in many children with Down syndrome prevent them from hearing speech sounds properly and cause them to say the sounds incorrectly. Children who suffer from frequent ear infections might hear the word "pretty" as "putty." Thus, they would risk misunderstanding or even ridicule by statements such as "The kitty is putty."

Most children learning to speak use immature phonological (sound) patterns, but usually these take on the adult form by age five to seven. However, children with Down syndrome tend to use these immature speech patterns much longer. This sometimes makes it more difficult to understand what they are saying, a problem that can hinder social interaction. One parent explains:

> When I go out and no one else can understand him or I go to pick him up at the nursery school and I hear the other kids saying things . . . I think, "Gee, my son knows everything you know, kid, he just can't say it." I've gotten to the point where I brag about him . . . because I want people to know that he's smarter than he seems because of his poor speech.[19]

Many children with Down syndrome who have speech difficulties work with speech therapists who help them practice forming and saying individual sounds. These sessions, called articulation exercises, often result in improved intelligibility, making communication much easier.

Even more significant is the ability to use and understand language. People use language to express their needs, to gain information, and to form and maintain relationships. Imagine being lost but unable to communicate that you need help. Imagine sitting

A hearing-impaired child with Down syndrome plays with a friend. Children with Down syndrome often understand more than what they are able to express.

alone on a playground, not knowing what words to use simply to introduce yourself to a group of classmates. Such scenarios can and do happen to children with Down syndrome, who frequently understand much more language than they know how to express.

Although there are many options available for enhancing the development of children with Down syndrome, the challenges the children face, from walking to making friends, are daunting to their parents. The opportunity to determine during pregnancy whether Down syndrome is present in the fetus gives parents a chance to learn ahead of time what these developmental difficulties are. Just how parents choose to deal with this knowledge is the subject of a heated ethical debate.

Chapter 3

The Screening Dilemma: To Live or Not to Live

DOCTORS MAY NOT understand what causes the extra chromosome of trisomy 21, but they do know enough about Down syndrome to identify fetuses that are likely to be carrying the disorder. Several prenatal (before birth) tests exist that can determine the risk of Down syndrome occurring. None of the tests are 100 percent accurate (although some are close), and some pose a health risk to either the mother or the baby. As a result, such screening tests are only performed when the mother exhibits a risk factor.

The decision to undergo a screening test for Down syndrome is a very personal choice. When Down syndrome is diagnosed, some parents opt to end the pregnancy, while others accept the challenge of raising a special-needs child and learn as much as they can about the disorder before the baby is born. The ethics of aborting fetuses with Down syndrome has sparked a debate about the value and quality of life for persons who have Down syndrome.

Who Is at Risk for Down Syndrome?

The most common risk factor is maternal age. Since the late 1800s doctors have noticed the increased rate of Down syndrome births to mothers thirty-five years or older. While the medical community is not sure why older mothers are more likely to have babies with Down syndrome, they think the risk is related to abnormalities in the eggs of older women. The risk of having a baby with Down syndrome is 1 in 370 births for women over the age of thirty-five. By contrast the risk at age twenty is only 1 in 1600 births.

Certain Down syndrome patients have one of two unusual forms of the disorder. About 3 to 4 percent have translocation, that is, the extra chromosome 21 attaches itself to another chromosome, usually chromosome 14, forming a single new chromosome. Genetic tests of parents who have babies with translocation sometimes show that one of the parents also has two chromosomes stuck together. Although the parent does not show any symptoms of Down syndrome, he or she is considered to be a "translocation carrier." If the carrier is the mother, the risk of having another child with Down syndrome is 12 percent, while if it is the father the risk is 3 percent.

An even smaller percentage, about 1 percent, are born with mosaicism, which occurs when something goes wrong in the first cell divisions after conception. Errors in chromosome divisions occur more frequently in children whose mothers are over the age of thirty-five at the time of conception. Because the error happens after the first few cell divisions have already taken place, only some of the baby's cells will have an extra chromosome while the rest will be normal. Many persons born with mosaicism have less pronounced characteristics of Down syndrome.

Once a parent has a child with Down syndrome, there is a 1 percent chance that other children will be born with the disorder as well. Physicians often encourage screening tests for couples when one or more of these risk factors is present.

Types of Screening Tests

Once it has been determined that a baby is at risk for having Down syndrome, based on the mother's age, the parents' genetic tests, or family history, the type of screening test must be selected. Since the 1960s several prenatal screening tests have been developed that are capable of determining the risk of Down syndrome. Today there are four main prenatal tests available, with varying rates of accuracy.

The least-invasive procedure is the use of ultrasonography, which involves sending sound waves into the womb, where they

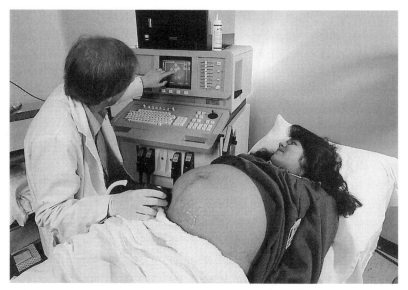

An ultrasound scan can sometimes determine if a baby will be born with Down syndrome.

bounce off the fetus. These sound waves are recorded on a monitor screen and then studied for any abnormalities. The thickness of the neck and the length of the leg bone can be measured, which may indicate features associated with Down syndrome. Any abnormalities in the heart may also indicate Down syndrome. However, these results are not always indicative of Down syndrome and may cause false alarms. In addition, a fetus that does have Down syndrome can have a normal ultrasound.

Another safe and relatively painless test is alpha-fetoprotein screening, a test that measures the level of alpha-fetoproteins (AFPs) in the mother's blood. AFPs are made in the fetal liver, and some get into the mother's blood. Because fetuses with Down syndrome are often smaller and have smaller placentas (the organ that attaches the baby's umbilical cord to the mother's uterine wall), lower levels of these proteins are associated with increased risk of Down syndrome. The accuracy rate with AFP screening is about 60 to 80 percent. Thus, a woman with abnormally low levels of AFPs can still have a child without Down syndrome.

Sometimes when screening by ultrasound or AFP indicates the possibility of Down syndrome, a woman will want to undergo a more definitive test. One such test is chorionic villus sampling (CVS), a more invasive and risky procedure that gives much more accurate results. Done during the eighth to eleventh week of pregnancy, CVS consists of inserting a hollow instrument through the vagina into the uterus, where a tiny piece of the placenta is suctioned. Cells from the placenta are then analyzed under a microscope for chromosomal abnormalities, which may indicate Down syndrome. The risks of CVS include infection to the mother, injury to the fetus, and miscarriage, although all are relatively uncommon.

The fourth common prenatal screening test, amniocentesis, is done somewhat later than CVS, usually around the fifteenth week of pregnancy. During amniocentesis, which is performed under local anesthesia, a long needle is inserted through the mother's abdomen into the womb, and a sample of amniotic fluid (fluid surrounding the fetus in the womb) is suctioned. In a laboratory, fetal cells are separated from the fluid and allowed to grow for two weeks. At this time, they can be analyzed for chromosomal abnormalities. As with CVS, amniocentesis carries with it risks of maternal infection, injury to the baby, or miscarriage. Amniocentesis is 99.8 percent reliable in diagnosing Down syndrome.

Since thirty-nine out of forty women who undergo either amniocentesis or CVS receive the good news of negative results, parents have to decide if the risks of the procedures are worth the peace of mind of knowing for sure. In fact, the availability of testing results early in pregnancy has raised an ethical controversy surrounding the decisions parents make when test results are positive for Down syndrome.

Knowing the Road Ahead

Many parents who get a screening done for Down syndrome simply want to know what challenges lie ahead of them in the event that a special-needs child is born. For some couples the thought of enduring several months of pregnancy wondering if the baby will be born with a disorder is excruciatingly painful. If the result is negative, they can breathe a sigh of relief and await the baby's birth with confidence. If they find out their baby has a high chance of being born with Down syndrome, they can take the next few months to familiarize themselves with the disorder, learning as much as possible about how they can help their child as he or she grows up.

There are also couples, those who are at highest risk due to family members with the disorder or a maternal age over thirty-five, who decide not to have any testing done. "Claire chose not to have the pre-natal testing the doctor suggested because she has a sibling with Down syndrome. I would have," said her mother, Marilyn Trainer, "But having a prenatal test is such an intimate, personal decision for a married couple . . . and so are any options that may follow."[20] The reason Claire decided not to undergo CVS was because she knew she would keep the baby whether or not it was born with Down syndrome. And having a

A doctor reviews the results from an amniocentesis and ultrasound with a patient. Knowing what challenges lie ahead allows parents to prepare themselves.

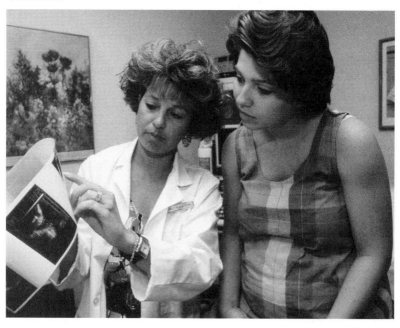

brother like Ben, who has Down syndrome, made her feel prepared to handle raising a special-needs child.

The Value of Life

What about parents who not only opt to have the prenatal screening done, but, in the case of a positive test for Down syndrome, choose to end the pregnancy? Because there is no proven treatment for Down syndrome some doctors and genetic counselors, expressing concern for the child's quality of life, indeed suggest this option. Often parents who choose to terminate a pregnancy believe that every baby has a right to be born healthy. A pediatrician who was faced with the prospect of giving birth to a child with Down syndrome explains her decision to end the pregnancy:

> [I] have taken care of several kids with DS [Down syndrome], some since birth, and it has been a very bittersweet experience which definitely influenced me to do the fetal reduction [abortion]. All of them have been very retarded [although] they have very sweet and loving dispositions. Two have had major cardiac surgeries. Two families have had divorces, mainly due to the increased stresses of taking care of the affected child. . . . [T]hese experiences helped me decide to do what I did.[21]

Nevertheless, there is a growing consensus among other doctors, human rights activists, and many parents of children with Down syndrome that chromosomally abnormal fetuses should not be aborted as if they were "defective goods." The outcome of every pregnancy is at least to some extent unexpected, and there are some who argue vigorously that parents do not have the right to choose life or death for a baby that would not be "up to specs." Moreover, although parents of children with Down syndrome acknowledge the many challenges of raising a special-needs child, they also insist that having a child with Down syndrome is not necessarily a negative experience.

Brett, the father of Amy, a little girl with Down syndrome, explains why he feels raising a special-needs child can be a positive experience:

Although Amy has needs which require our time, attention and resources, (to some this constitutes a burden), she too gives to us, and she does this freely, generously and without expectation. Her "gift" of humanity, her gentle spirit and enthusiasm for living offers a community the chance to see beyond the "outer wrapper" of disability to the person within. She and children like her provide us opportunities to realize that there are dimensions to the human experience that transcend our beliefs about gender, race, intelligence or physical perfection.[22]

Amy was diagnosed with Down syndrome by means of a series of prenatal screening tests, and her parents used the remainder of the pregnancy to learn as much as they could about the disorder. "Because Amy's diagnosis occurred during pregnancy," Brett said, "I knew a lot about my child before she was born."[23] Not only was he able to prepare himself for caring for a

A six-year-old boy with Down syndrome spends time with his father. Parents of Down syndrome children feel that raising a special-needs child can be a positive experience.

baby with Down syndrome, but knowing beforehand allowed him to work through the initial negative emotions of grief, guilt, shame, anger, denial, and confusion. By the time Amy was born, Brett was physically and emotionally better prepared to deal with a child who had Down syndrome.

Amy's parents never considered abortion; they welcomed their daughter, just as they knew she would be. Yet at the time of discovery, either when test results return positive or a baby is born with the disorder unexpectedly, almost all parents are left reeling in shock and sadness. "I was like a little kid," said one parent, upon learning that her newborn had Down syndrome. "I wanted to say 'take it away, take it back,' but I knew it wouldn't go away." [24]

Thus it is understandable that when the emotionally vulnerable moment of discovery occurs during a pregnancy, not all couples are able to marshal the psychological and material resources required of the parents of a special-needs child. Moreover, opponents of the abortion option believe that many parents are pressed into making a quick decision because the earlier the procedure is done, the less the risk to the woman undergoing it. "We decided to terminate the pregnancy after just one night of 'deliberations,'" explains one parent. "We are not that young (35), and have another child. Those were the major two factors prompting us to make the choice we did make. I would also have hated to see my child suffer in any way, knowing what problems are associated with DS [Down syndrome]." [25] In some cases ultrasounds show that the baby is developing with physical abnormalities that are incompatible with life. Faced with the knowledge that their child would very likely live in pain and probably die in infancy, some parents decide to end the pregnancy and prevent the suffering of their baby.

Not Without a Doubt

The choice whether or not to undergo prenatal screening is a very personal decision, as is the choice to terminate a pregnancy or bring a child with Down syndrome into the world. But as for these children, there seems little doubt that life is a worthwhile undertaking for them. As writer Claire D. Canning, whose daughter has Down syndrome, expresses:

> I feared so for our new little child, Martha. This was surely not the life I had intended to give her. But I have learned that her life is very precious, that she is singularly happy . . . with a degree that makes me wonder just what constitutes "normality.". . . The child with Down syndrome does almost everything a normal child does, but more slowly. . . . They will walk, and run, and laugh, and tell you when they are thirsty or hungry. They usually will be able to read and write, will love school and music, and will delight in travel. They will swim, bowl, take ballet lessons, join Boy Scouts or Girl Scouts, take sailing, horseback riding, and piano lessons, go to camp . . . among so many other things we might wish for all our children. . . . They will be bundles of mischief, imps with sticky fingers, and, only incidentally, children who happen to have handicaps. Unlike our other children, they will love us unconditionally . . . with a resolve . . . that almost defies understanding.[26]

Children with Down syndrome share with other children the same enjoyment in recreational and physical activities such as swimming.

Those parents who accept the challenge of raising a child who has Down syndrome are called on to provide great amounts of love, patience, and understanding. Forming partnerships with their local public schools and community programs can enhance the opportunities they give their children for developing to their potential.

Chapter 4

Growing Up with Down Syndrome

GROWING UP, CHILDREN with Down syndrome do many of the same things normal children do. They go to school, see movies, play, attend camps, participate in sports events, and enjoy hobbies. However, this is a far cry from the days when special education in public schools was just beginning. A law called the Individuals with Disabilities Education Act (IDEA) was passed in 1975 (under the original title Education for all Handicapped Children Act), guaranteeing a "free and appropriate public education" for all children with disabilities. IDEA also requires that students with disabilities get services to meet their individual needs from the ages of three to twenty-one years.

Today the focus is on helping children with Down syndrome grow up to be as independent as possible. Schools and communities develop educational programs and enrichment opportunities that help these children and their families achieve this goal. There are programs available that enhance the overall development of children with Down syndrome from infancy through the young adult years.

Early Intervention: A Head Start in Life

Babies and toddlers with Down syndrome often get a jumpstart in their overall development through early intervention programs. Early intervention is special instruction or therapy designed to help children with disabilities such as Down syndrome improve motor skills, social skills, language skills, and cognitive skills. "Early intervention taught Ricky a lot of important foundation skills," explained one parent. "[Such as] paying attention, understanding what school time meant, finishing a task, and responding to requests."[27] The people who deliver these services are teachers, physical or occupational (fine motor) therapists, and speech therapists.

Often these professionals come to the home of infants to work with them in a familiar place surrounded by family members. Toddlers may receive services at a hospital center or at a school. Sometimes the center is a better choice for toddlers because they have the opportunity to interact with other children there and begin to work on social skills. The skills children with Down syndrome work on in early intervention give them a foundation for further learning and social interaction when they begin formal schooling, usually in preschool or kindergarten. This is illustrated in a vignette described by an early childhood education professional: "Shannon enjoys wiping up her own spills with a sponge and scrubbing the table after snack. She is involved in the natural consequence of cleaning up which fosters an understanding of personal responsibility."[28]

Going to School: Special Education

When children with Down syndrome enter preschool or kindergarten in public schools they begin learning in two different ways. One is called functional learning, which is learning self-help skills like dressing, feeding, and toilet training. The other is academic learning, including formal instruction in reading and math. As children with Down syndrome grow older and progress through school, the focus shifts more and more away from academics and toward functional learning. The

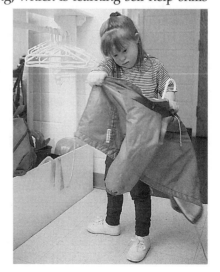

Special education programs help children master the basic skills needed in everyday life.

reason for this is because they need to be responsible as much as possible for meeting their own needs if they are to live independently as adults. For a young adult with Down syndrome it is more important to know how to balance a checkbook than to understand algebra, just as it is more important to be able to read and fill out a job application than to read Shakespeare's plays.

This is not to say that academics are not important; they are. However, most education professionals do not believe it is useful for children who have reached their maximum potential in a skill to spend additional time drilling at that level. Most children with Down syndrome learn to read and write, but the average level is at second grade. Some achieve third- or fourth-grade-level skills, while a few may achieve even higher. Many children who have Down syndrome endure great frustration in school, as their slower rate of reading and writing can affect their ability to finish a test, read a history book, or understand a science experiment. When Jason Kingsley was in high school, he wrote about the distress these frustrating experiences caused:

> [W]hen I'm in school, I write slowly and when I write fast my writing comes sloppy and people don't understand my writing. . . . When I'm slow I keep behind. . . . After the bell rings . . . I may not be finished and do the things for homework which I hate to do. . . . I'm lucky because I'm doing my homework at lunchtime and at study hall. If the bell rings from there, what can I do? I just have to do it at home, and I hate that. I'm very slower than anyone. I'm slower than most people. . . . I wish I was faster. . . . I want them to stop so I can catch up. I don't want teachers to go faster than I am, too. I want people to have the same pace as I do. I want everyone to . . . learn the same. . . . I may not be able to learn things and that makes me have a hard time. I still have a disability. How I want it to get away.[29]

Math seems to be more difficult for many children with Down syndrome. About half master second-grade-level math skills, while the rest never advance beyond the first-grade level. This means that they can learn basic adding and subtracting, but skills such as multiplication and division are usually out of their reach.

Active participation in school helps a Down syndrome child develop academic and social skills. Here, a preschooler gives a presentation on the weather.

However, a calculator can be used to compensate for these limitations. Learning to use such a tool may allow them to manage their own money in shopping, banking, and budgeting later as adults.

Like other children, those with Down syndrome do not all learn exactly the same way or achieve the same functional or academic skill levels. Because individual needs and abilities vary from person to person, schools must create an Individual Education Program (IEP) for each student with Down syndrome. An IEP states what a child needs to learn, how he or she will learn these skills, and who will help him or her achieve them. It also states where the learning is to take place.

Mainstreaming

Where students who have Down syndrome learn is the subject of an important debate among educators and parents. Learning may take place either in a special education classroom or in a regular classroom. Placing students with Down syndrome in a regular education classroom for part or all of the school day is called mainstreaming. Marquita Grenot-Scheyer, a professor of education at California State University, Long Beach, describes how a special-needs student might be mainstreamed in a regular education activity:

> Carla and her classmates are engaged in building a castle with sugar cubes, glue, sequins, and other art materials as part of the class unit on classic fairy tales. Although Carla, a third-grade student with Down syndrome, does not like the sticky feeling of glue, she does enjoy working with her peers and listening to them read . . . the story. Together Carla's group has delegated work responsibilities for the day. Carla agreed to be responsible for distributing and collecting materials and to provide suggestions regarding the design of the castle. It was okay with Carla and her peers if she did not want to get involved in the actual construction of the castle. Later . . . an instructional assistant helps Carla write a short entry for her journal on what life in a castle might have been like.[30]

Children with Down syndrome may spend all day in a regular classroom with special service providers, such as speech or physical therapists, coming into the classroom. These same service providers may opt to work with the children elsewhere, away from the other students. Usually though, children with Down syndrome are assigned to a self-contained classroom, where a special education teacher works only with special education students. Not all the students in the self-contained classroom will have Down syndrome, and not all of them will be working on the same skills or have the same needs. Usually the special education teacher gives formal instruction in reading and math and also works on functional skills, such as self-feeding and dressing.

Often children with Down syndrome will spend time in a regular education classroom during art, social studies, science, or physical education activities. Usually they will also intermingle with the other students at lunch and recess and during school functions like assemblies. This gives them the opportunity to socialize with children who do not have special needs. It is important for children with Down syndrome to observe children with normal social

Most parents of children with Down syndrome feel that mainstream education for their child is beneficial.

and language development interacting because such experiences give them practice in socializing in the "real world." Marilyn Trainer explains how mainstreaming benefited her son:

> It was our doctor who first suggested that we try to get Ben into a nursery school with "normal" children. She thought that if he could get the maximum exposure to normal children, be a part of their activity each day, and, most important, be exposed to their developing speech, it would help his own development. . . . The children . . . had good feelings about Ben. . . . He was very popular. When he was absent they missed him and asked about him. . . . Ben was in the school for over two years. In that time his vocabulary increased beyond measure, his independence grew so that his favorite phrase was, and still is, "I'll do it!" And he became completely toilet trained, even at night. We have never had any doubt that sending Ben to a normal nursery school was the right decision for us.[31]

Most parents of children with Down syndrome believe mainstreaming is beneficial to their child. They also believe that giving other children the chance to interact with peers who have

Down syndrome allows them to develop acceptance of people who have disabilities. Some parents and teachers oppose mainstreaming outright charging that special needs tend to be overlooked and that students with Down syndrome are often neglected in the regular classroom. Moreover, there is no guarantee that other students will always accept their special-needs classmates and treat them with respect, as Jason's story shows:

> Middle school was difficult. . . . [P]eople teased me because they think that is fun. They said words to me that I don't like. They called me names. I'm not comfortable when people tease me. . . . When it's time to do my Science test, some . . . people did make noise during the test so I couldn't concentrate. . . . But I did okay.[32]

Among parents who have reservations about mainstreaming, some do not believe in it at all, while others admit it is good for social development but are not certain that children with Down syndrome are learning anything else. One parent said, "Our son

Some parents feel that while mainstreaming is good for the development of social skills, it does not help children with Down syndrome.

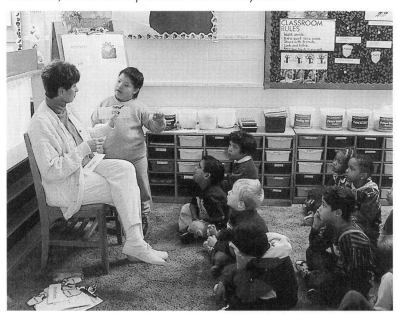

is . . . not ready for a . . . regular classroom. He's going to have up to fifteen hours a week with the special resource people. So he'll be out of his regular classroom getting some help with reading and writing, language, speech, and that kind of thing. What we're doing is creating a 'buddy system' with regular education students."[33] However, even if mainstreaming is limited, children with Down syndrome have many opportunities to mingle with nondisabled people through recreation and work in their communities.

Community Integration

Children with Down syndrome can find many opportunities to interact with others through organized groups, events, or lessons that include people with disabilities. Youth clubs and recreation programs provide classes in sports and arts and crafts. For example, the YMCA and YWCA offer swimming lessons, summer camps, and a variety of classes in arts or other hobbies. The Boy Scouts and Girl Scouts of America are open to children with Down syndrome as well. Houses of worship may also offer activities or events that are appropriate for children with Down syndrome.

Children with Down syndrome play at the park, hang out with neighborhood kids, and go to play groups just like other children. They also go to the mall, see movies in theaters, browse through museums, and attend concerts and sports events. Jason describes the many activities of his middle school years:

> I went to Camp Lee-Mar. I met some friends there. . . . I was a camper-worker. The first job I did was sorting out the mail. The second job I did was sorting out the silverware. And my third job was teaching little kids . . . how to use a computer, how to use a pencil, then teach them how to write postcards every Sunday. . . . I also practiced the piano . . . I played kid songs and Mozart and Bach. That was a time that I knew the composers by then—Bach, Brahms, Tchaikovsky, Beethoven, Mozart. And I started to love Broadway musicals. . . . I practically know all the Broadway shows. . . . I listen to them in the car . . . [and] love to sing along.[34]

Many children with Down syndrome take dance or music lessons, painting classes, or develop other hobbies.

Various groups, classes, or sports provide ample opportunity for social interaction. Here, a young girl with Down syndrome participates in a dance class.

Older children and teenagers with Down syndrome often participate in Special Olympics, an international sports program for people with developmental disabilities. Special Olympics promotes athletics, teamwork, and self-esteem among people with developmental disabilities, as Christi Todd, a young woman who has Down syndrome, attests:

> When I was 10, my teacher . . . taught me gymnastics and introduced me to Special Olympics. . . . I was able to participate in my high school gymnastics program and I actually assisted my classmates with their routines. It made me feel great! . . . I have also competed in swimming, diving, basketball, and bowling. I've even tried a little golf. I am currently learning to ride horses. It's a lot like being on a balance beam, except the horse moves and hopefully I do not! Special Olympics has had a tremendous influence on my life. [It] has given me the opportunity to train and compete and prove to my family and friends what I can do. This makes them proud of me and I am proud of myself. . . . Through Special Olympics, people are given the opportunity to get off the sidelines and participate in life.[35]

The Special Olympics are currently developing an integrated program called Unified Sports, where disabled and nondisabled athletes work together as teammates.

Some high schools provide opportunities for students with Down syndrome to participate in regular school sports through a partners' club. The club consists of nondisabled students who give individual coaching assistance that allows special-needs athletes to play on the school's regular team. Such programs build self-esteem and promote acceptance of disabled persons in the community. The highly publicized story of Gabe Lane's 1996 fight to play on his Greeley, Colorado, high school football team is an example of the partners' club in action. A college student volunteered to go to every practice and game and helped Gabe with personal coaching throughout the summer before football season began. After a legal battle with a state agency, Gabe was able to play in several games, going with his team all the way to the division championships.

Sporting events such as the Special Olympics help promote teamwork and self-esteem among developmentally disabled persons.

Giving a child with Down syndrome the opportunity to participate in the community allows the child to develop individual interests and to grow as a person. It also gives valuable practice in social skills with peers and with community members like store clerks, bus drivers, or police officers. Moreover, by integrating with the community, children with Down syndrome not only educate the public about their disorder but also make it clear that they are people first and that their disability is secondary.

Chapter 5

Preparing for Adulthood

MOST TEENAGERS EXPERIENCE the frustration of being in between childhood and adulthood. Teens and young adults with Down syndrome are no exception, and in many cases must work especially hard to make the transition from dependence to independence. Like most teens and young adults, those with

A teenager with Down syndrome participates in a mainstream art class. Mainstream high school classes help teens with Down syndrome acquire the skills necessary to live independent lives.

Down syndrome want to make choices about friends, dating, work, and how they spend their leisure time. Many make goals for themselves that include a career, marriage, and getting a driver's license. Often, however, these choices are limited by individual capabilities, leading to great frustration for many teens with Down syndrome. "Sometimes I have conflict between everything I do," explains Jason Kingsley. "I'm right between a kid or a man. I'm right between what my mom wants and what my dad wants. Panic, tragedy. Where my life is going to. . . . I am always trying hard to do [the] best I can."[36]

During the high school years, many parents and teachers put increased emphasis on vocational training, daily living skills, and social skills in an effort to make this transition as successful as possible. Even after leaving the public school system, an adult with Down syndrome may obtain further job and independent living skills training through residential programs. Despite the existence of such programs, limited funding and space often mean long waiting periods for those who need these services in order to make the transition to independent living.

Self-Reliance and Prevocational Training in High School

When Shauna entered the ninth grade she found herself spending most of her time in a classroom with other special-needs students. Her teacher spent the mornings working with her on functional academics—reading and math skills used in practical situations—such as reading laundry instructions and adding prices while grocery shopping. During the afternoons Shauna focused on practical living skills, like hygiene and other self-care skills, care of her personal belongings, and interaction in the community, including shopping, transportation, and time management. She also practiced social skills through role playing with her teacher and classmates. Her favorite parts of the day, however, were lunch and physical education class when she could spend time with her "buddy group," a group of girls her age who ate lunch every day with Shauna and included her in their extracurricular activities.

In the eleventh grade Shauna began prevocational (job preparation) training, which helped with her transition from school to the adult world of working and independent living. On-the-job training is important for teenagers with Down syndrome in several ways. By experiencing a variety of jobs, they may be better able to decide what type of work they want to do after they graduate from high school. Work experience in school also provides an opportunity for students with Down syndrome to learn appropriate work habits and social skills in a job setting. Achievement of such skills is an important indicator of future success in employment. The importance of developing good

Vocational training allows students with Down syndrome to learn job skills that will help them develop self-reliance.

communication skills at work is underscored in this story by writer H. D. Bud Fredericks:

> A young man who was working in an animal hospital and who was normally friendly and outgoing would come to work and would not greet his fellow employees. The employees, most of whom had never had experience with persons with Down syndrome, were acquiring negative feelings toward all people with Down syndrome because of the apparent unfriendliness of this student. The veterinarian pointed this out . . . [and] learned that the student did not speak to the fellow employees because he could not remember their names. [They] solved the problem by taking Polaroid pictures of each of the employees and then role played with the student using the pictures, which helped the student remember the names.[37]

Usually when a student with Down syndrome undergoes vocational training, he or she will spend from three to ten hours per week on the job. A school employee acts as a job coach, supervising the student at work and training him or her in the job responsibilities. Being able to hold a job after graduating from high school provides a measure of self-sufficiency, which is paramount to achieving independence as an adult with Down syndrome.

Besides prevocational training, high school students with Down syndrome also learn practical living skills. Shauna and her classmates often take field trips to various places in their community, such as the grocery store, a shopping mall, the bank, the post office, the theater, or local recreation center. On each of these trips, Shauna practices skills such as asking and answering questions of clerks, managing money, making lists, addressing mail, choosing a leisure activity, and taking public transportation, like a bus. Mastering such skills helps those with Down syndrome take more responsibility for their own needs.

"Why Can't I Be Like Everyone Else?"

For teenagers who have Down syndrome, these years when peer approval and social interaction are so important can be full of increased frustration as well as wonder and excitement. More than ever, having appropriate social skills is essential. Likewise, inability to discern people's motives can make those with mental retardation vulnerable to thieves, con artists, or others who might take advantage of them. As a result, even as teenagers, youth with Down syndrome are seldom allowed to go out—with or without friends—unsupervised by responsible adults.

To some extent the degree of frustration that teens with Down syndrome experience depends on the level of mental retardation. Those with mild retardation (IQs between 55 and 70) can participate more in peer activities but will also be more aware of their limitations than those with moderate retardation (IQs between 40

A teenage girl visits a music store with her friends. Most teens with Down syndrome long to "be like everyone else."

and 55). Marilyn Trainer describes the dilemma for a friend's daughter who had Down syndrome but functioned at almost a "normal" level:

> [She] is actually taking driver education in school and so far is passing the course. She spends hours every night doing the homework required, homework it takes the other students fifteen minutes . . . to do. [She] is absolutely determined to drive a car. . . . She is "mainstreamed" in a regular high school and longs to have friends who are in the "normal" population, to be one of them. She reads romance novels and yearns for a romance of her own, with a non-disabled boyfriend. This teenager has told her mother that she thinks people with Down syndrome are "ugly," and she doesn't want "to have it." [She also says,] "I hate Down syndrome! I hate being mentally retarded! Why can't I be like everyone else?"[38]

Likewise, Trainer's son Ben had a friend who also had Down syndrome but who wanted to date "normal" girls. "Why won't they go with me?" he asked. "How come they always say no?"[39] He had trouble understanding why he was not accepted like other boys his age.

On the other hand, romance can and does happen for teens with Down syndrome, although usually between two teens who are both mentally retarded. Writer Claire D. Canning's daughter Martha arrived home from high school one day and announced that a classmate in her special education class had asked her to the homecoming dance. Canning chaperoned the dance so she could watch over Martha and her date from a distance. Later Canning recalled another romantic incident: "One young man in Martha's class called her 'sweetheart,' and she beamed. At the school bus stop, they held hands, and, ever so gently, he kissed her—and she loved it. . . . [T]hese two young adults enjoyed a kiss on a spring afternoon!"[40]

Sometimes when teens with Down syndrome feel left out, peer rejection may not be the issue. The young woman who was taking driver's education also wanted to have "normal" friends, but often conversations would get over her head and she would end up feeling confused and frustrated. The other girls talked with her and tried to include her, but they could not always keep their conversations at her level of understanding. This was not because they rejected her but because at times the need of the majority to communicate on a higher level could not be avoided.

Teens and young adults with Down syndrome are frequently more trusting of others than is prudent. They tend not to question what others want them to do and often fail to foresee the consequences of such actions. Mitchell Levitz says of an experience in high school:

> When I was influenced to set off the fire alarm . . . I was suspended for five days. . . . I can understand that this was very serious, but [later] . . . both of my sisters were there to tell me not to listen to those people because they can get you into serious trouble. By having both of them there, they helped me realize that I can make friends who understand me for who I am.[41]

Just as Mitchell relied on his sisters to help him make choices about friends, many teens with Down syndrome benefit from having a trustworthy peer or adult who can guide them away from unscrupulous persons and deter them from acts having antisocial aspects beyond their understanding. Ironically, this dependence on others to help make judgment choices can get in the way of the desire to be self-reliant.

To Be, or Not to Be, Independent

The reality for most teenagers with Down syndrome is that they will do many of the same activities other teens do, but they do so mostly with mentally retarded peers and usually under supervision. While most normal teenagers choose their friends and where they want to work and gain independence by getting a driver's license, such choices may be limited for those with Down syndrome. "Ben will make few such choices," said Trainer. "He has a job he likes very much, but he didn't choose it. We found it for him, filled out the applications. . . . We did the choosing."[42]

A matter of particular importance to teens and young adults with Down syndrome is driving. Just as it is for other teens, being able to drive is one of the most significant statements of independence from one's parents. Some do learn to drive and earn their license, as Brenda Lynn Bargmann, a public speaker who has Down syndrome, explains: "Last November [1998], I received my driver's license on my first try. I was so happy and excited! Three weeks ago, I was given a Pontiac station wagon by a friend. Mom won't let me drive it alone yet, but 'Look out, here I come!'"[43]

On the other hand, some individuals, like Ben Trainer, do not have sufficient motor or mental skills to operate a car safely, while others are limited in their ability to assess a situation quickly and resolve it safely, as would be necessary to avoid another vehicle that suddenly spins out of control. As Jason illustrates, "It's so hard to talk about. . . . I need special skills to drive, to learn easily. . . . You got to study for a couple of years. . . . You got to get your judgement. . . . Sometimes a child who has Down syndrome can lose his judgement a little because they're not learning as much as . . . expected."[44] In many communities people like Jason and Ben can use public transportation to get where they want to go without having to rely on others for a ride.

Residence Programs

Although there are many programs available to young adults with Down syndrome to help ease the transition from school to work, often these programs are understaffed and underfunded. Most programs have long waiting lists. This means that many end up waiting months, or even longer, to get the training they need in vocational and independent living skills.

When entering a residence program, the young adult with Down syndrome begins learning workplace skills like time management and communication, and job-seeking skills such as completing job applications and speaking at an interview. Moreover, residents learn to take care of themselves, from cooking, cleaning, and arranging transportation to simple money management. In many cases, recreational activities are provided. Mitchell describes his experience at one such residence program:

These young adults live in a resident home for disabled persons. Residence programs help many people with Down syndrome by teaching them how to make decisions for themselves.

[I'm] being able to continue my skills by joining a residence program down in South Orange, New Jersey, where I have most of my friends . . . and they will give me some knowledge that I achieved certain skills already, but I need to practice more of these skills to continue on the path to the future. Now I am on a waiting list until an apartment is open and when I am accepted to move in, I am able to continue on with my future. . . .

When an apartment opens up, then I am able to move into the apartment with four or five other people. . . . Also there are certain chores that have to be done and each person does a certain chore each day, such as cooking, cleaning, shopping. . . .

And the other part is to be able to hold your money and to be able to use a budget. . . . The people who are in charge of the program go out and find a job the person is interested in . . . they will tell the person that they found a job that is fit for you and you go into that job and get started. . . . You get paid for the job . . . they may have a van or a bus to take you to the job. . . .

After work, they do certain activities. . . .They may have dances, they will go to basketball games . . . and they also probably go to wrestling matches down in New York. They take a van or a bus . . . to get you to these events.[45]

The transition to adulthood proceeds most smoothly when young adults who have Down syndrome are encouraged to make as many choices as possible for themselves. Today there are a variety of work and residence options available to accommodate the needs and desires of a wide range of capabilities among adults with Down syndrome.

Chapter 6

Living and Working with Down Syndrome

MITCHELL LIVES ON his own, has a job, and hopes one day to get married. His friend Jason has similar goals. Like many young adults today, people with Down syndrome are graduating from high school, working, and striving for independence. However, much of this is accomplished with help from government and community programs and these young people's own families. As Mitchell and Jason learned, the skills needed to live independently can take years and a lot of practice to attain for people who have Down syndrome.

With support and time, some adults with Down syndrome are making decisions about where they want to live, who they want to live with, and where they want to work. They also choose how to spend

A woman with Down syndrome vacuums her room at a group home.

their leisure time and who their friends are, even though this usually means joining a group with other disabled adults. Some are even marrying. Today more adults than ever before who have Down syndrome are living a full and productive mainstream life and are working toward new goals for themselves as individuals and as advocates for people with disabilities.

Finding a Job

Although there are scores of job placement and training programs scattered throughout the nation, there are not nearly enough to serve all the eligible disabled persons. Waiting lists are usually quite long, and there is no guarantee that a program will find a job for every adult with Down syndrome.

Sometimes families themselves must find the jobs for their adult children with Down syndrome, as Marilyn Trainer and her husband did for their son, Ben. When Ben was faced with months of waiting to get into any sort of vocational training program, they took matters into their own hands, scouting around the community, gathering job applications, and seeing that they were filled out properly. Finally they found him a position at a local grocery store as a courtesy clerk.

When starting a new job a person with Down syndrome is often accompanied by a job coach. The coach supervises the new employee and helps train him or her in the job responsibilities. A job coach will stay until the employee with Down syndrome can perform his or her duties independently, which could be anywhere from a few days to a few months. "The job coach, a gentle, patient, retired psychologist . . . helped Ben for two weeks," said Trainer. "By then it was apparent that Ben didn't really need a job coach anymore. [The] store manager . . . felt that Ben could take directions perfectly well from store personnel."[46]

To Hire or Not to Hire

Once placed in a job, a person with Down syndrome tends to be a hardworking, loyal employee. In Oklahoma, a survey found that 96 percent of employers were happy with the work performance of mentally retarded employees, and over half were satisfied with their productivity (how much work they get done). One would think, based on these figures, that businesses would be eager to hire persons with Down syndrome. However, the reality is that only about 35 percent of slightly mentally retarded persons are employed. Why?

One reason is that vocational programs cannot accommodate everyone who needs their services, and many adults with Down syndrome do not get the help they need in training and job placement. Another reason is that many employers are simply not aware of the benefits of hiring people with Down syndrome. In many cases fear that they will turn away customers or pose a safety hazard in the workplace is to blame. "I soon found out that despite a lot of positive publicity about hiring the handicapped, there is no plethora [abundance] of jobs," explained Trainer. "And you had better believe that many people in positions of authority are still reluctant to hire someone with mental retardation, no matter how great the publicity."[47]

Mitchell Levitz, a man with Down syndrome who, along with other advocates for the rights of the disabled, has traveled to Washington, D.C., numerous times to lobby for improved job opportunities, outlines the needs of adults with Down syndrome.

> When I went on the [Capitol] Hill, me and a couple of other people spoke to . . . congressional leaders. . . . I raised the issue of employment because I feel that people with developmental disabilities and mental retardation need opportunities to have a job, to work in competitive employment. And I stressed the impact of having more funding to create more jobs. . . . From my perspective, it makes good business sense to have people of this kind of nature to work in these . . . position[s] because they have the right to work, to earn money, to make a living of their own. . . . They should be nondiscriminatory toward mental and physical disability. . . . We want people to have jobs, to earn money because it's part of the goal that everyone needs. To have the chance to be successful, to have a chance to work in the environment where other people are working.[48]

Yet another reason for the lack of employment among adults with Down syndrome is low pay. Often jobs that persons with

Down syndrome can handle pay at the low end of the scale. However, usually even working adults who have Down syndrome are eligible to receive Supplemental Security Income (SSI) and Social Security Disability Insurance (SSDI) from the federal government. Both SSI and SSDI provide financial assistance and are based on the type of disability as well as the level of income. Thus a fear voiced by some parents and advocates—that income support from government programs will be stopped if the person goes to work—is largely groundless.

All in a Day's Work

The level of income greatly depends on the type of work available. There are three types of employment in which persons with Down syndrome may work. The first, competitive employment, is the best paying and most desirable because it consists of regular jobs in the

community that are worked by either disabled or nondisabled persons. Such jobs include animal caretaker, building maintenance worker, library assistant, data entry clerk, medical technician, store clerk, cook, appliance repair assistant, or housekeeper. Mitchell Levitz describes several jobs he held while in a residency program right after high school:

> My first job . . . [was] at the Assemblywoman Maureen Ogden's. I work[ed] in her office as a clerical aide. Part of my job [was] to file and to open the mail and to

Vocational programs try to find competitive, steady employment for persons with Down syndrome.

stamp them. I also stamp[ed] booklets to be put out in the office. . . . [Now] I am working at Summit Trust as a bulk teller. . . . Part of my job at Summit Trust is to sort coins, re-bagging, and to write the ticket that goes on the bag of coins. I also do the microfilming [of] batches of checks and sometimes I help my supervisor Eileen by bringing the money to the drive-up. . . . I have a second job and it is part-time. I work at Pizza Hut. . . . My responsibilities at the job are [to] prep garlic bread and clean off and refill the salad bar. Then I became the manager of the dishwasher. . . . The people who I work with are very nice to me and they feel very comfortable with me working there.[49]

A person with Down syndrome might also work in supported employment, where he or she is paid to work with other disabled persons or alone, supervised by a job coach. This type of arrangement works best with those who need considerable help in learning and performing the job duties.

The third type of workplace is a sheltered workshop, which is a segregated setting where all the employees are disabled (not necessarily with Down syndrome). Because there is no integration, many states are phasing out sheltered workshops or turning them into training centers where the employees will eventually be transferred to competitive employment.

Competitive employment offers the best opportunity to be wholly or partially self-sufficient. Self-sufficiency is an important step toward living independently in a desired type of residence.

A Home of One's Own

There are a variety of ways adults with Down syndrome can live either independently or semi-independently, whether in an apartment, a house, or a group home. A group home is a residence where up to six individuals live together with a twenty-four-hour support staff on duty. The group home arrangement is very popular among persons with Down syndrome, but waiting lists are extremely long. "Years ago . . . we put Ben's name on several waiting lists for group homes in our area," explained Trainer. "There is no reason to think, though, that they're going to have a

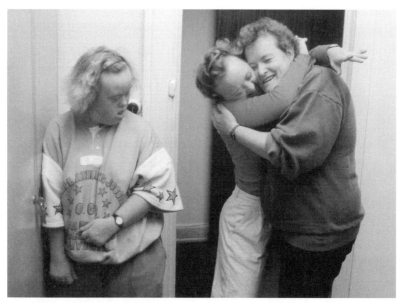

A woman with Down syndrome hugs a caretaker. While some people with Down syndrome live by themselves, others require some level of supervision.

place for him any time soon; the waiting lists are long and emergency situations are considered first."[50]

Some, like Mitchell Levitz, are striving to live on their own with as little support as possible. As a young adult nearly two years out of high school, Mitchell explained what his goals were for independent living:

> At the present time, I'd like to live on my own. If I decided, on down the road, that I want to have a roommate, I'll decide then. First I'd like to have an apartment by myself. Then later, if the time is right, I would like other people to move in with me. When I get settled in first and get comfortable, and know what I'm doing, then I'll be relaxed and won't have any [stress] by having other people to live with at the same time. But I'd like it to be my choice . . . I do have some experience of being in a single apartment. Right now I have a roommate. He's nice and everything . . . but now I feel the time is right . . . to begin to have my own privacy. To have a single room and then have a single apartment.[51]

Of course not everyone with Down syndrome is able to make the choices that Mitchell describes. Some individuals who are lower functioning must depend more on others to get their needs met. Some have more serious health problems that require round-the-clock or frequent care. No matter what the level of care may be, many adults with Down syndrome are making choices about who they live with, whether it is roommates, family members, or even a spouse.

Marriage and Children?

Today many people with Down syndrome are getting married, although few have children because of reproductive problems related to the disorder. Adults with Down syndrome do fall in love and get married, usually to another person who has a developmental disability or mental retardation. Sometimes the marriage is arranged by the two individuals' families, who take on the responsibility of setting the couple up in their own home and looking after their more complex needs.

Married couples who are capable of functioning for long periods of time without supervision may live alone in their own apartment or house (often provided by family members). For those who need more assistance, someone who provides guidance and support in areas of need may live with the couple or stop by and check in with them every day.

Self-Determination

More than anything, young adults with Down syndrome want to make decisions about their own lives. In many cases this is possible, but personal limitations put decision making in some areas out of reach.

Jason Kingsley votes; Ben Trainer does not. Why do these two young men, similar in many respects, differ here? Jason studies the political campaigns, has opinions about how the government should be run, and has even participated in forming public policy through meeting with legislators as an advocate for people with disabilities. In contrast, Marilyn and Allen Trainer decided not to register Ben to vote. Marilyn explains:

Ben has the legal right to vote. But he would have absolutely no idea whom to vote for: issues and candidates would be completely over his head. . . . Someone who goes into a voting booth should know what he or she is doing and understand what the process is truly about. We also know that an unscrupulous person could easily take advantage of Ben in urging him to vote one way or another.[52]

Sometimes adults with Down syndrome need someone to make financial or medical decisions for them. Usually this falls to the parents or a legal guardian. The guardian's authority is limited to certain matters, as prescribed by the courts. For example, Sue, a young woman who has Down syndrome, lives in a group home with several other disabled adults. She makes her own personal decisions, chooses her jobs, shops on her own, and plans her leisure time herself. But her sister, who acts as her legal guardian, is responsible for making decisions about Sue's health care. This is important because Sue has kidney problems that might require hospitalization, and a hospital would need informed consent before beginning a procedure that could either save her life or jeopardize it. Because of her disability, however, Sue is not legally competent to give informed consent, and so she needs someone who understands the benefits and risks of the treatment in question to accept or reject the hospital's plan.

Similarly, a guardian may be responsible for investing money, managing a bank account, and protecting the assets of an adult with Down syndrome who can otherwise manage the rest of their own affairs. In some cases a guardian may be appointed to make personal decisions as well, although this is discouraged unless the individual with Down syndrome is too low functioning to be capable of deciding where to work, where to live, and who to live with.

Self-Advocacy

Today more people than ever before who have Down syndrome are fighting for their rights. This effort of speaking up for their own interests is called self-advocacy and has helped to build self-confidence and independence among many adults with Down syndrome. The goals of these advocates are echoed in this essay written by Mitchell Levitz:

> Our dream is to fight for inclusion for all and to make it work. . . . We want to be treated with dignity and respect and that is important to us. That is why we must tell the members of Congress to take a better look at IDEA. . . .
>
> We need people to focus on our abilities and capabilities. We need to work together as a TEAM. That is what the organization I work for, Capabilities Unlimited, does. We believe by working together as a TEAM we can make a difference.
>
> . . . I am the Editor-in-Chief of a newsletter called the Community Advocacy Press. It is a newsletter written by people with disabilities about issues important to us. I'll bet that the doctors never would have thought that we would be able to write and publish a newsletter. I'll also bet the doctors never thought our . . . families would support us to be leaders in our community. That is why people like us want to make a difference and that is why I say "inclusion for all."[53]

Advocacy is important because, although great strides have been made toward integrating individuals with Down syndrome in the community, there is still a long way to go. There are still people and places that hold on to old notions and prejudices about mental retardation. There are also still people that believe persons with mental retardation should be segregated in schools and the community. When such attitudes are prevalent, they severely limit opportunities for people with Down syndrome to develop their potential and become contributing members of society.

Advocates make themselves heard through public speaking, writing for publication, and working with legislators to improve and create policies that benefit the disabled. Chris Burke, the star of television's *Life Goes On*, works as the editor in chief of *News & Views*, a magazine for and about individuals with Down syndrome and their families. He also acts as the Goodwill Ambassador for the National Down Syndrome Society, a position that allows him to speak with other youths who have Down syndrome

Actor Chris Burke (who has Down syndrome) works as an advocate for people with this condition.

and encourage them to work hard and recognize their capabilities. "In addition to talking to young people," wrote Burke, "I speak to parents and teachers and legislators. I tell legislators how important it is to support services for children so they can grow up to be independent and good citizens."[54]

Medical researchers, doctors, educators, and advocates all share with affected families the goal of seeing persons with Down syndrome grow up to be independent citizens. As the work to improve opportunities for people with Down syndrome continues, science continues its pursuit of a cure for this disorder.

Chapter 7

Current Trends: Looking Toward the Future

THERE ARE MANY studies being done in genetic research and biochemistry that are striving to find a way to prevent Down syndrome from occurring, or at least to reverse its effects. The best known research is being conducted through the Human Genome Project, which is attempting to identify genes in the human body. Other alternative treatments are nutritional intervention and cell therapy, both considered experimental but popular with many parents of children with Down syndrome. Finally, there is a continuing effort to educate the public about Down syndrome and to promote awareness regarding the dignity and contributions of those who were born with this condition.

The Human Genome Project

The Human Genome Project is an ongoing research effort conducted by scientists all over the world. The project's goals are to name the genes on all twenty-three chromosome pairs in the human body and to determine what characteristic each gene is responsible for. By doing this, scientists are creating a "genetic map" that shows the path from gene and chromosome to genetic expression (actual characteristic) in a living person, animal, or plant. For example, researchers might discover that a certain gene on a particular chromosome is responsible for the color of human eyes.

A scientist working on the Human Genome Project examines some samples. Knowledge gained from this work may lead to treatments for Down syndrome.

Currently a global team of scientists is working together to decode the genes on chromosome 21, in hopes of determining which are responsible for the characteristics of Down syndrome. By 1999 about 20 percent of the genes on chromosome 21 had been identified. Scientists hope to decode the rest of chromosome 21's genes early in the twenty-first century.

The information gleaned from the Human Genome Project may be used to treat Down syndrome in two ways. First, if the function of the gene is known, this function may be manipulated through changes in body chemistry using drugs or diet. Second, even if the function is not known, the work of the genes in chromosome 21 may be decreased to stop the harmful effects of having 50 percent too much "expression." In other words, scientists might not know which gene causes heart defects in persons with Down syndrome. However, they do know that, whatever the gene, three copies of it have heart problems. Since every gene contributes 50 percent of the genetic expression of a particular trait, if there are three copies of the heart function gene or 150 percent total, the heart condition probably will be present. If doctors could decrease the gene function by 33.3 percent then the heart problem might be avoided.

Medical practitioners all over the world are using this information to develop treatments for Down syndrome. Some of these treatments are controversial due to questions about the validity of studies done on them. Nevertheless, many parents and individuals with Down syndrome are taking a chance and trying these treatments out.

The Warner Program

Jack Warner is a pediatrician in Fullerton, California, who operates the Warner House, a center that studies Down syndrome and provides a therapy program. Dr. Warner's treatment consists of nutrition, metabolic therapy, physical therapy, and developmental optometry (vision).

Unlike Dr. Turkel before him, Dr. Warner tailors the nutrition and drugs used to fit the individual needs of the child. For instance, where Turkel routinely prescribed thyroid hormone to all patients, Warner does not prescribe the supplements for thyroid abnormality unless tests have revealed a need.

The nutritional part of Warner's treatment consists of custom-prescribed capsules called Hap Caps, which he claims will treat metabolic abnormalities. Warner's program is based on the concept of "50 percent too much expression" from the genetic hypothesis. Warner adds other drugs and thyroid supplements if a child's medical tests indicate they are needed. He usually refers his patients for physical therapy, family counseling, and optometry.

Warner claims that his treatments are successfully reversing some of the cognitive and physical symptoms of Down syndrome. He reports that intelligence and motor skills have improved, and that those children who started the program very early in life also have less pronounced physical features typical in Down syndrome.

However, the Warner treatment has not been tested in a double-blind study. In a double-blind study one group is given the actual treatment, while another, the control group, receives a placebo. To guard against possibly distorting psychological effects, neither the staff administering the drugs nor the participants of the study know which group they are in. After a certain amount of time on the treatment, the participants are observed, questioned, or tested to see if the treatment has had any effect, and to see if there are any differences between the placebo group and the control group.

Warner cites the validity of his treatment using an A-B-A-B study, which involves administering the therapy for a period of time (an A phase), discontinuing the treatment for a while (a B phase), returning to the therapy (another A phase), and so on, assessing changes and effects after each phase. "The teachers will write to us and say that the treated children with Down syndrome are more motivated. . . . One mom said that the teacher could tell when she ran out of the Hap Caps," said Ardith Meyer, the Warner program physical therapist. "The child went right back to being lethargic and uninterested."[55]

Although Warner's program has not been determined to be a proven treatment for Down syndrome due to the lack of double-blind studies, hundreds of parents have sought treatment for their children at his center. Moreover, his work in nutritional therapy has contributed to the development of another, similar treatment.

Targeted Nutritional Intervention

The use of nutrition to battle the effects of Down syndrome has most recently been developed as a therapy called Targeted Nutritional Intervention (TNI). TNI attempts to correct nutritional imbalances caused by the metabolic abnormalities in Down syndrome. The supplements used consist of vitamins, minerals, amino acids, and digestive enzymes.

Chris Wills used TNI with his daughter Ellie, who was born with Down syndrome in 1996. Ellie began the treatment when she was four months old, and at the age of one year she could understand and comply with simple requests such as "Ellie give me that." Her motor skills continued to be delayed, however, as she was fourteen months old when she began to crawl (seven to nine months is average). "At the time of writing, Ellie is 17 months old," Wills wrote months later. "Apart from being perhaps a little behind in her fine motor skills, in all other respects she seems to be not far from following a virtually 'normal' developmental curve."[56]

Past research casts doubt on parents' claims that TNI and other nutritional therapies are successful. In a double-blind study done in 1983, twenty individuals with Down syndrome received vitamin supplements. The study revealed no significant differences between the placebo and control groups in appearance, growth, or health. Moreover, high doses of some vitamins have been proven to have harmful side effects, such as skin rashes, bone disorders, and seizures. On the other hand, proponents of TNI point out that the 1983 study and others with similar findings only used vitamins, without the other metabolic substances TNI uses.

In spite of the risks and the lack of conclusive studies supporting nutritional therapy, parents continue to use supplements like TNI. Why? "From my perspective," said Wills, "the prospect that this sort of nutritional intervention might prevent the premature degeneration of cell tissue, and particularly the degeneration of brain cells in my child was very persuasive."[57]

In addition to using nutritional supplements, many individuals with Down syndrome are increasingly taking "nootropics," which are drugs that are designed to improve brain function.

Smart Drugs

Chris Wills's daughter Ellie was not only being treated with TNI but was also taking a nootropic drug called piracetam. Piracetam is increasingly being used to improve intellectual performance, and research indicates it may stimulate the central nervous system and protect cells from oxidation (lack of oxygen). Although there are no reported side effects, no studies have yet been done on the effects of piracetam or any other nootropics on people with Down syndrome.

Madison, a little girl with Down syndrome, began taking nutritional supplements and piracetam as a toddler. Her mother,

Scientific advances combined with greater human compassion and understanding will improve the quality of life for all people with Down syndrome.

Dixie Lawrence, reported that "after Madison first went on piracetam, she spontaneously potty-trained herself, started speaking in phrases, and developed an active symbolic imagination."[58]

With the increasing popularity of piracetam use for enhancing intelligence in children with Down syndrome, researchers are expressing interest in conducting studies on it in the near future. Such studies, if their results support parental claims, could open a door to reversing the mental retardation effects of Down syndrome in the future. In the meantime, piracetam remains unapproved by the Food and Drug Administration, although it may be legally imported from foreign sources for personal use. In addition, the medical community cautions parents of children with Down syndrome to be aware of the risks and benefits of using this unproven drug.

Besides the use of nutritional supplements to change the effects of Down syndrome, other even more controversial therapies are being studied as possible alternative treatments. These investigations are conducted mainly in Europe, where governmental requirements for the testing of treatments applied to humans are less strict than in the United States. In any event, no large double-blind studies have been performed to allow the medical community to thoroughly assess the alternative treatments, and it is unlikely that they will be available in the United States in the near future.

Every Single One of Us Counts

As genetic information is made available at the fingertips of doctors around the world, there is great hope that Down syndrome can be prevented. As scientists learn more about how this disorder affects the human body there is also a chance that a truly effective treatment to reverse the effects of Down syndrome will be developed.

But genetic engineering alone will not improve the quality of life for people with Down syndrome in the twenty-first century. Society must also develop greater compassion for people with Down syndrome, and strive to include them in numerous, diverse aspects of the community. Mitchell Levitz describes what he envisions the future to be for those who have Down syndrome:

> You're an individual, an adult with a disability, who can handle any issue, tackle any issue. It's part of being an adult, knowing who you are, understanding who you are. Because we are people who understand, knowing about our disability. People can change, people can realize you are an individual and an identity is important to you, to your family, even to your community. People consider you an individual with rights. People respect you for who you are. Not just your disability. . . . That's what counts. . . . We are individuals and they [society] are counting us in. . . . Every single one [of us] counts because we are an important asset in the community and they need our voice.[59]

Notes

Introduction: The Road to Acceptance
1. Jason Kingsley and Mitchell Levitz, *Count Us In: Growing Up with Down Syndrome.* New York: Harcourt Brace, 1994, p. 3.

Chapter 1: The History of Down Syndrome
2. Marilyn Trainer, *Differences in Common: Straight Talk on Mental Retardation, Down Syndrome, and Life.* Bethesda: Woodbine House, 1991, pp. 77–78.
3. Édouard Séguin, *Idiocy: And Its Treatment by the Physiological Method.* New York: William Wood, 1866, pp. 39–77.
4. Quoted in Siegfried M. Pueschel, *A Parent's Guide to Down Syndrome.* Baltimore: Paul H. Brookes, 1990, p. 36.
5. Quoted in Pueschel, *A Parent's Guide to Down Syndrome*, p. 36.
6. Trainer, *Differences in Common*, p. 91.
7. Quoted in Pueschel, *A Parent's Guide to Down Syndrome*, p. 38.
8. Trainer, *Differences in Common*, p. 31.
9. Quoted in Romayne Smith, ed., *Children with Mental Retardation: A Parent's Guide.* Bethesda: Woodbine House, 1993, p. 47.

Chapter 2: Growing and Developing with Down Syndrome
10. Trainer, *Differences in Common*, p. 14.
11. Trainer, *Differences in Common*, p. 217.
12. Quoted in Smith, *Children with Mental Retardation*, p. 76.
13. Quoted in Smith, *Children with Mental Retardation*, p. 196.
14. Trainer, *Differences in Common*, p. 180–81.
15. Quoted in Smith, *Children with Mental Retardation*, p. 18.
16. Quoted in Smith, *Children with Mental Retardation*, p. 18.
17. Quoted in Smith, *Children with Mental Retardation*, p. 294.
18. Quoted in Smith, *Children with Mental Retardation*, p. 81.

19. Quoted in Smith, *Children with Mental Retardation,* p. 74.

Chapter 3: The Screening Dilemma: To Live or Not to Live

20. Trainer, *Differences in Common,* p. 196.
21. Quoted in "Making the Decision to Interrupt." Available at www.erichad.com/ahc/DS1.htm.
22. Brett Chun, "A Father's Perspective." Available at www. fathersnetwork.org/web/articles/adv/chun.htm.
23. Chun, "A Father's Perspective."
24. Quoted in Pueschel, *A Parent's Guide to Down Syndrome,* p. 11.
25. Quoted in "Making the Decision to Interrupt."
26. Quoted in Pueschel, *A Parent's Guide to Down Syndrome,* pp. 3–6.

Chapter 4: Growing Up with Down Syndrome

27. Quoted in Smith, *Children with Mental Retardation,* p. 181.
28. B. Thompson et al., *The Process of Instruction: Facilitating Participation of Young Children with Severe Disabilities in Mainstream Early Childhood Programs.* Lawrence, KS: Learner Managed Designs, 1993.
29. Kingsley and Levitz, *Count Us In,* pp. 38–39.
30. Quoted in Terry J. Hassold and David Patterson, eds., *Down Syndrome: A Promising Future, Together.* New York: Wiley-Liss, 1999, p. 189.
31. Trainer, *Differences in Common,* pp. 5–7.
32. Kingsley and Levitz, *Count Us In,* p. 24.
33. Quoted in Smith, *Children with Mental Retardation,* p. 177.
34. Kingsley and Levitz, *Count Us In,* pp. 24–25.
35. Quoted in Hassold and Patterson, *Down Syndrome,* pp. 285–86.

Chapter 5: Preparing for Adulthood

36. Kingsley and Levitz, *Count Us In,* p. 152.
37. Quoted in Pueschel, *A Parent's Guide to Down Syndrome,* pp. 199–200.
38. Trainer, *Differences in Common,* p. 142.
39. Trainer, *Differences in Common,* p. 142.
40. Quoted in Pueschel, *A Parent's Guide to Down Syndrome,* p. 274.

41. Kingsley and Levitz, *Count Us In,* p. 50.

42. Trainer, *Differences in Common,* p. 158.

43. Quoted in Hassold and Patterson, *Down Syndrome,* p. 276.

44. Kingsley and Levitz, *Count Us In,* p. 144.

45. Kingsley and Levitz, *Count Us In,* pp. 166–67.

Chapter 6: Living and Working with Down Syndrome

46. Trainer, *Differences in Common,* p. 192.

47. Trainer, *Differences in Common,* pp. 188–89.

48. Kingsley and Levitz, *Count Us In,* pp. 139–40.

49. Kingsley and Levitz, *Count Us In,* pp. 152–53.

50. Trainer, *Differences in Common,* p. 218.

51. Kingsley and Levitz, *Count Us In,* p. 171.

52. Trainer, *Differences in Common,* p. 159.

53. Quoted in Hassold and Patterson, *Down Syndrome,* p. 282.

54. Quoted in Hassold and Patterson, *Down Syndrome,* p. 277.

Chapter 7: Current Trends: Looking Toward the Future

55. Quoted in Steven W. Fowkes and Ward Dean, "Smart Drugs and Down's Syndrome," *Smart Drug News,* February 14, 1994. Available at www.ceri.com/downs1.htm.

56. Chris Wills, "Targeted Nutritional Intervention (TNI)," *Down's Syndrome Association Newsletter,* July 1997. Available at www.downsyndromeresearch.force9.co.uk/tni.htm.

57. Wills, "Targeted Nutritional Intervention (TNI)."

58. Quoted in Fowkes and Dean, "Smart Drugs and Down's Syndrome."

59. Kingsley and Levitz, *Count Us In,* p. 180.

Organizations to Contact

The Arc (formerly the Association of Retarded Citizens)
National Headquarters
PO Box 1047
Arlington, TX 76004
(817) 261-6003
http://thearc.org

The Arc is one of the oldest organizations founded to serve the interests of people with mental retardation. It provides services in nearly every area of need, including education, family support, health care, community integration, and employment. The website offers an impressive question-and-answer section that covers a wide array of issues and provides resources for further information.

National Assocation for Down Syndrome (NADS)
PO Box 4542
Oak Brook, IL 60522-4542
(708) 325-9112
www.nads.org

This nonprofit organization offers membership to parents and professionals and publishes a newsletter and periodical, *NADS News*. NADS supports fundraising efforts and awareness programs for Down syndrome.

National Down Syndrome Congress
7000 Peachtree-Dunwoody Road, NE
Lake Ridge 400 Office Park Bldg. #5, Ste. 100

Atlanta, GA 30328
1-800-232-6372
www.ndsccenter.org/index3.htm<http://www.ndsccenter.org/index3.htm>

This nonprofit organization provides resources and information to parents and professionals on Down syndrome. It is dedicated to improving the lives and opportunities of individuals with Down syndrome by conducting fundraising and promoting awareness. It publishes a popular newsletter, *Down Syndrome News* and also holds national conventions every year.

The National Down Syndrome Society (NDSS)
666 Broadway
New York, NY 10012
www.ndss.org

This organization works for the interests of individuals with Down syndrome and their families, including education, research, and advocacy. The Society publishes a newsletter, and the website provides links to many international connections. The NDSS also holds national and international conferences relating to health education, community, and vocational issues affecting Down syndrome.

For Further Reading

Barbara Adams, *Like It Is: Facts and Feelings About Handicaps from Kids Who Know.* New York: Walker, 1979. This book covers a wide range of disabilities, but includes an informative chapter on mental retardation and developmental disabilities, including Down syndrome. It provides definitions of terms and useful information about, for example, IQ tests. It also explores the sometimes still-present fear, much less prevalent now than in 1979, of people who are mentally retarded as potentially dangerous.

Sheila Garrigue, *Between Friends.* Scarsdale, NY: Bradbury Press, 1978. This book presents the story of a young girl who develops a friendship with another girl who has Down syndrome. It explores social attitudes and relationships between "normal" and mentally retarded peers.

Lynn Nadel and Donna Rosenthal, eds., *Down Syndrome: Living and Learning in the Community.* New York: John Wiley and Sons, 1995. This book offers current information on programs available that help people with Down syndrome participate in community life. Topics include achieving independence, family support, sibling relationships, development, health care advances, education, and employment. Each section is introduced with a commentary written by an adult with Down syndrome.

Robert Perske, *Circle of Friends.* Nashville, TN: Abingdon Press, 1988. This book houses a collection of heartwarming true stories about friendships between people with disabilities and those who are "normal." It explores the issue of acceptance and demonstrates how such friendships can flourish regardless of race, age, or ability.

Karin Schwier, *Speakeasy: People with Mental Handicaps Talk About Their Lives in Institutions and in the Community*. Austin: Pro-Ed, 1990. This book provides firsthand accounts from mentally retarded adults who describe their experiences living in institutions or other segregated places. By contrast, there are also stories about their lives in their communities and how integration affected them.

Salvatore Tocci, *Down Syndrome*. New York: Franklin Watts, 2000. This book, written for older children and teens, provides a good overview of all aspects relating to Down syndrome, including history, education, community integration, employment issues, advocacy, and some current experimental treatments.

Works Consulted

Books

Terry J. Hassold and David Patterson, eds., *Down Syndrome: A Promising Future, Together.* New York: Wiley-Liss, 1999. This book offers a broad range of information, including the most recent research in medical, vocational, educational, and developmental issues. It includes informative chapters that discuss some of the current controversial alternative treatments for Down syndrome, including nutritional therapy and smart drugs. The end of the book presents several short essays written by adults with Down syndrome.

Jason Kingsley and Mitchell Levitz, *Count Us In: Growing Up with Down Syndrome.* New York: Harcourt Brace, 1994. This book is actually a transcript of conversations with Kingsley and Levitz, two friends who have Down syndrome. The recordings, made while Kingsley and Levitz were in high school, cover their thoughts and feelings about their disability, education, independence, relationships with friends and family, dating, sexuality, marriage, religion, politics, and their individual goals for the future.

Siegfried M. Pueschel, *A Parent's Guide to Down Syndrome.* Baltimore: Paul H. Brookes, 1990. This book includes a chapter on the history of Down syndrome, as well as one that explains the genetics behind the disorder. It also covers the topics of education and mainstreaming, development, vocational training and opportunities, community integration, and special concerns for teens with Down syndrome.

Édouard Séguin, *Idiocy: And its Treatment by the Physiological Method.* New York: William Wood, 1866. This book provides an interesting look at how the medical community viewed mental retardation in the nineteenth century. Although much of the scientific narrative is out-of-date and incorrect, the text is full of references to treating mentally retarded people with respect and descriptions of the benefits of educating them. Includes one of the earliest descriptions of Down syndrome ever recorded.

Romayne Smith, ed., *Children with Mental Retardation: A Parent's Guide*. Bethesda: Woodbine House, 1993. This book includes a comprehensive look at mental retardation, including social, developmental, educational, vocational, and integration issues, and a chapter covering some of the major causes of mental retardation, including Down syndrome. Information is provided on legal concerns and advocacy as well. Each chapter section includes quotes from parents of mentally retarded children.

B. Thompson, D. Wickham, J. Wegner, M. M. Ault, P. Shanks, and B. Reinertson, *The Process of Instruction: Facilitating Participation of Young Children with Severe Disabilities in Mainstream Early Childhood Programs*. Lawrence, KS: Learner Managed Designs, 1993. This work includes a good section on mainstreaming special-needs children in early childhood programs, including information on philosophy, methods of communicating and encouraging participation, and meeting individual needs in the classroom.

Marilyn Trainer, *Differences In Common: Straight Talk on Mental Retardation, Down Syndrome, and Life*. Bethesda: Woodbine House, 1991. This book consists of numerous essays written by Trainer reflecting on the experiences of her son, Ben, who has Down syndrome. The author presents the challenges of living with this disability in a sensitive, sometimes humorous, and down-to-earth style. Topics include the language of disability, advocacy, independence, vocational issues, peer relationships, and how people with Down syndrome view themselves.

Periodicals

D. Hernandez and E. M. C. Fisher, "Down's Syndrome Genetics: Unraveling a Multifactorial Disorder," *Human Molecular Genetics*, vol. 5, 1996, pp. 1411–16.

Academic Paper

Paul J. Benke, Virginia Carver, and Roger Donahue, "Risk and Recurrence Risk of Down Syndrome," University of Miami School of Medicine, October 1995. This paper explains the types of Down syndrome and gives statistics on the risk of recurrence of each one. It also provides a description of four major screening tests for Down syndrome, including accuracy rates and risks.

Internet Sources

Brett Chun, "A Father's Perspective." Available at www. fathersnetwork.org/web/articles/adv/chun.htm.

"Earlier Screening for Down Syndrome?" *Health News*, October 26, 1998. Available at www.onhealth.com/ch1/in-depth/ item/item,25428_1_1.asp.

Steven W. Fowkes and Ward Dean, "Smart Drugs and Down's Syndrome," *Smart Drug News*, February 14, 1994. Available at www.ceri.com/downs1.htm

"Making the Decision to Interrupt." Available at www.erichad. com/ahc/DS1.htm.

Chris Wills, "Targeted Nutritional Intervention (TNI)," *Down's Syndrome Association Newsletter*, July 1997. Available at www.downsyndromeresearch.force9.co.uk/tni.htm.

Index

Picture Credits

Cover photo: Photo Researchers/Richard Hutchings
Bettmann/Corbis, 18
Corbis/Laura Dwight, 31, 38
Corbis/Anne Griffiths Belt, 36
Corbis/Miki Kratsman, 66
Corbis/Stephanie Maze, 61, 63, 68
Corbis/Joseph Sohm; Chromo Sohm, Inc., 51
FPG, 15
FPG/Ron Chapple, 9, 25, 29, 43, 45
FPG/Terry Qing, 34
Impact Visuals, 74
Photofest, 72
Photo Researchers, 57, 78
Photo Researchers/Richard Hutchings, 47, 53
Photo Researchers/Andy Levin, 24, 40
Photo Researchers/Lawrence Migdale, 17
Photo Researchers/Elaine Rebman, 50
Photo Researchers/Ellen B. Senisi, 48
Photo Researchers/Lily Solmssen, 55
Photo Researchers/Erika Stone, 22
Photo Researchers/L. Willat, 19
Photo Researchers/Susan Woog-Wagner, 13

About the Author

Christina M. Girod received her undergraduate degree from the University of California at Santa Barbara. She worked with speech- and language-impaired students and taught elementary school for six years in Denver, Colorado. She has written scores of short biographies as well as organizational and country profiles for educational multimedia materials. The topics she has covered include both historical and current sketches of politicians, humanitarians, environmentalists, and entertainers. She has also written *Native Americans of the Southeast* for Lucent's Indigenous Peoples of North America series. Girod lives in San Diego, California, with her husband, Jon Pierre, and daughter, Joni.